This Journal Belongs To:

____

"Traveling leaves you speechless,

then turns you into a storyteller."

- Ibn Battuta

Visit Us
www.enchantedwillowco.com

Date: ______________

Weather:

From: ______________

To: ______________

Route Taken: ______________

Beginning Mileage:

Ending Mileage:

Total Miles Traveled:

Campground Information

Name: ______________

Address: ______________

Phone: ______________

Site # ______ $ ______ ☐ Day ☐ Week ☐ Month

☐ First Visit	☐ Return Visit	☐ Easy Access	
☐ Site Level	☐ Back-in	☐ Pull-through	
☐ 15 amp	☐ 30 amp	☐ 50 amp	
☐ Water	☐ Sewer	☐ Shade	☐ Sun
☐ Paved	☐ Sand / Grass	☐ Gravel	
☐ Picnic Table	☐ Fire ring	☐ Trees	☐ Lawn
☐ Patio	☐ Kid Friendly	☐ Pet Friendly	
☐ Store	☐ Cafe	☐ Firewood	
☐ Ice	☐ Security	☐ Quiet	☐ Noisy

Our Rating: ☆ ☆ ☆ ☆ ☆

GPS: ______________

Altitude: ______________

Cell Service / Carrier: ______________

☐ Antenna Reception ☐ Satellite TV ☐ Cable TV

☐ WIFI Available ☐ Free ☐ Fee $ ______

Memberships: ______________

Amenities: ______________

Location	☺ 😐 ☹	Water Pressure ☺ 😐 ☹
Restrooms	☺ 😐 ☹	Laundry ☺ 😐 ☹
Pool	☺ 😐 ☹	Hot Tub ☺ 😐 ☹

Places Visited / Activities:

People Met / New Friends:

Food, Dining & Restaurants:

Highlights / Memorable Events:

Places To Go & Things To Do for Next Time:

Notes:

Date: ____________

Weather:

From: ____________

To: ____________

Route Taken: ____________

Beginning Mileage: ____________

Ending Mileage: ____________

Total Miles Traveled:

Campground Information

Name: ____________

Address: ____________

Phone: ____________

Site # ________ $ ________ ☐ Day ☐ Week ☐ Month

☐ First Visit ☐ Return Visit ☐ Easy Access

☐ Site Level ☐ Back-in ☐ Pull-through

☐ 15 amp ☐ 30 amp ☐ 50 amp

☐ Water ☐ Sewer ☐ Shade ☐ Sun

☐ Paved ☐ Sand / Grass ☐ Gravel

☐ Picnic Table ☐ Fire ring ☐ Trees ☐ Lawn

☐ Patio ☐ Kid Friendly ☐ Pet Friendly

☐ Store ☐ Cafe ☐ Firewood

☐ Ice ☐ Security ☐ Quiet ☐ Noisy

Our Rating: ☆ ☆ ☆ ☆ ☆

GPS: ____________

Altitude: ____________

Cell Service / Carrier: ____________

☐ Antenna Reception ☐ Satellite TV ☐ Cable TV

☐ WIFI Available ☐ Free ☐ Fee $ ________

Memberships: ____________

Amenities: ____________

Location ☺ 😐 ☹ Water Pressure ☺ 😐 ☹

Restrooms ☺ 😐 ☹ Laundry ☺ 😐 ☹

Pool ☺ 😐 ☹ Hot Tub ☺ 😐 ☹

Places Visited / Activities:

People Met / New Friends:

Food, Dining & Restaurants:

Highlights / Memorable Events:

Places To Go & Things To Do for Next Time:

Notes:

Date:	From:	Beginning Mileage:
Weather:	To:	Ending Mileage:
	Route Taken:	Total Miles Traveled:

Campground Information

Name:

Address:

Phone:

Site # $ ☐ Day ☐ Week ☐ Month

☐ First Visit	☐ Return Visit	☐ Easy Access	
☐ Site Level	☐ Back-in	☐ Pull-through	
☐ 15 amp	☐ 30 amp	☐ 50 amp	
☐ Water	☐ Sewer	☐ Shade	☐ Sun
☐ Paved	☐ Sand / Grass	☐ Gravel	
☐ Picnic Table	☐ Fire ring	☐ Trees	☐ Lawn
☐ Patio	☐ Kid Friendly	☐ Pet Friendly	
☐ Store	☐ Cafe	☐ Firewood	
☐ Ice	☐ Security	☐ Quiet	☐ Noisy

Our Rating: ☆ ☆ ☆ ☆ ☆

GPS:

Altitude:

Cell Service / Carrier:

☐ Antenna Reception ☐ Satellite TV ☐ Cable TV

☐ WIFI Available ☐ Free ☐ Fee $

Memberships:

Amenities:

Location	☺	😐	☹	Water Pressure	☺	😐	☹
Restrooms	☺	😐	☹	Laundry	☺	😐	☹
Pool	☺	😐	☹	Hot Tub	☺	😐	☹

Places Visited / Activities:

People Met / New Friends:

Food, Dining & Restaurants:

Highlights / Memorable Events:

Places To Go & Things To Do for Next Time:

Notes:

Date: ______ From: ______ Beginning Mileage: ______

Weather: To: ______ Ending Mileage: ______

Route Taken: ______ Total Miles Traveled: ______

Campground Information

Name: ______ Our Rating: ☆ ☆ ☆ ☆ ☆

Address: ______ GPS: ______

Phone: ______ Altitude: ______

Site # ______ $ ______ ☐ Day ☐ Week ☐ Month

Cell Service / Carrier: ______

☐ First Visit	☐ Return Visit	☐ Easy Access	
☐ Site Level	☐ Back-in	☐ Pull-through	
☐ 15 amp	☐ 30 amp	☐ 50 amp	
☐ Water	☐ Sewer	☐ Shade	☐ Sun
☐ Paved	☐ Sand / Grass	☐ Gravel	
☐ Picnic Table	☐ Fire ring	☐ Trees	☐ Lawn
☐ Patio	☐ Kid Friendly	☐ Pet Friendly	
☐ Store	☐ Cafe	☐ Firewood	
☐ Ice	☐ Security	☐ Quiet	☐ Noisy

☐ Antenna Reception ☐ Satellite TV ☐ Cable TV

☐ WIFI Available ☐ Free ☐ Fee $ ______

Memberships: ______

Amenities: ______

Location	☺	😐	☹	Water Pressure	☺	😐	☹
Restrooms	☺	😐	☹	Laundry	☺	😐	☹
Pool	☺	😐	☹	Hot Tub	☺	😐	☹

Places Visited / Activities:

People Met / New Friends:

Food, Dining & Restaurants:

Highlights / Memorable Events:

Places To Go & Things To Do for Next Time:

Notes:

Date: ____	From: ____	Beginning Mileage: ____
Weather:	To: ____	Ending Mileage: ____
	Route Taken: ____	Total Miles Traveled:

Campground Information

				Our Rating: ☆ ☆ ☆ ☆ ☆		
Name: ____				GPS: ____		
Address: ____				Altitude: ____		
Phone: ____				Cell Service / Carrier: ____		
Site # ____	$ ____	☐ Day ☐ Week	☐ Month	☐ Antenna Reception	☐ Satellite TV	☐ Cable TV
☐ First Visit	☐ Return Visit	☐ Easy Access		☐ WIFI Available	☐ Free ☐ Fee	$ ____
☐ Site Level	☐ Back-in	☐ Pull-through		Memberships: ____		
☐ 15 amp	☐ 30 amp	☐ 50 amp		Amenities: ____		
☐ Water	☐ Sewer	☐ Shade	☐ Sun	Location	Water Pressure	
☐ Paved	☐ Sand / Grass	☐ Gravel		Restrooms	Laundry	
☐ Picnic Table	☐ Fire ring	☐ Trees	☐ Lawn	Pool	Hot Tub	
☐ Patio	☐ Kid Friendly	☐ Pet Friendly				
☐ Store	☐ Cafe	☐ Firewood				
☐ Ice	☐ Security	☐ Quiet	☐ Noisy			

Places Visited / Activities: ____

People Met / New Friends: ____

Food, Dining & Restaurants: ____

Highlights / Memorable Events: ____

Places To Go & Things To Do for Next Time: ____

NOTES:

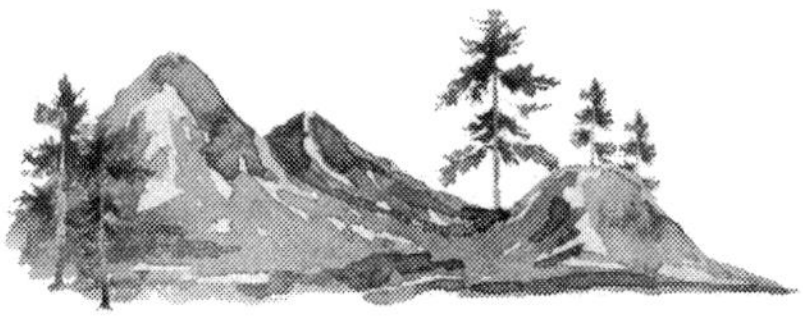

Date: ____	From: ____	Beginning Mileage: ____
Weather:	To: ____	Ending Mileage: ____
	Route Taken: ____	Total Miles Traveled:

Campground Information

Name: ____
Address: ____
Phone: ____
Site # ____ $ ____ ☐ Day ☐ Week ☐ Month

☐ First Visit	☐ Return Visit	☐ Easy Access	
☐ Site Level	☐ Back-in	☐ Pull-through	
☐ 15 amp	☐ 30 amp	☐ 50 amp	
☐ Water	☐ Sewer	☐ Shade	☐ Sun
☐ Paved	☐ Sand / Grass	☐ Gravel	
☐ Picnic Table	☐ Fire ring	☐ Trees	☐ Lawn
☐ Patio	☐ Kid Friendly	☐ Pet Friendly	
☐ Store	☐ Cafe	☐ Firewood	
☐ Ice	☐ Security	☐ Quiet	☐ Noisy

Our Rating: ☆ ☆ ☆ ☆ ☆
GPS: ____
Altitude: ____
Cell Service / Carrier: ____
☐ Antenna Reception ☐ Satellite TV ☐ Cable TV
☐ WIFI Available ☐ Free ☐ Fee $ ____
Memberships: ____
Amenities: ____

Location	Water Pressure
Restrooms	Laundry
Pool	Hot Tub

Places Visited / Activities:

People Met / New Friends:

Food, Dining & Restaurants:

Highlights / Memorable Events:

Places To Go & Things To Do for Next Time:

Notes:

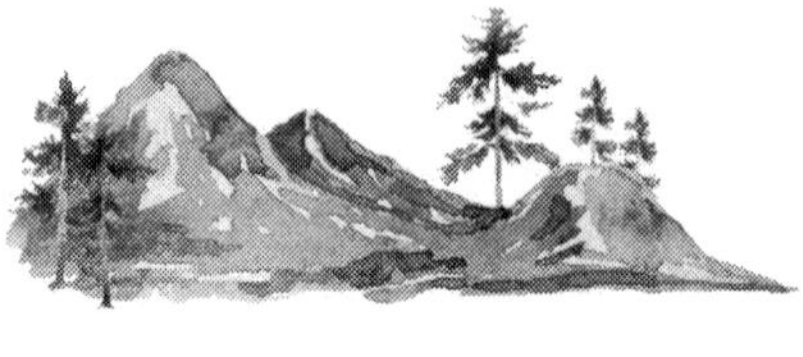

Date: ______________

Weather:

From: ______________

To: ______________

Route Taken: ______________

Beginning Mileage: ______________

Ending Mileage: ______________

Total Miles Traveled:

Campground Information

Name: ______________

Address: ______________

Phone: ______________

Site # ________ $ ________ ☐ Day ☐ Week ☐ Month

☐ First Visit ☐ Return Visit ☐ Easy Access

☐ Site Level ☐ Back-in ☐ Pull-through

☐ 15 amp ☐ 30 amp ☐ 50 amp

☐ Water ☐ Sewer ☐ Shade ☐ Sun

☐ Paved ☐ Sand / Grass ☐ Gravel

☐ Picnic Table ☐ Fire ring ☐ Trees ☐ Lawn

☐ Patio ☐ Kid Friendly ☐ Pet Friendly

☐ Store ☐ Cafe ☐ Firewood

☐ Ice ☐ Security ☐ Quiet ☐ Noisy

Our Rating: ☆ ☆ ☆ ☆ ☆

GPS: ______________

Altitude: ______________

Cell Service / Carrier: ______________

☐ Antenna Reception ☐ Satellite TV ☐ Cable TV

☐ WIFI Available ☐ Free ☐ Fee $ ________

Memberships: ______________

Amenities: ______________

Location ☺ 😐 ☹ Water Pressure ☺ 😐 ☹

Restrooms ☺ 😐 ☹ Laundry ☺ 😐 ☹

Pool ☺ 😐 ☹ Hot Tub ☺ 😐 ☹

Places Visited / Activities:

People Met / New Friends:

Food, Dining & Restaurants:

Highlights / Memorable Events:

Places To Go & Things To Do for Next Time:

NOTES:

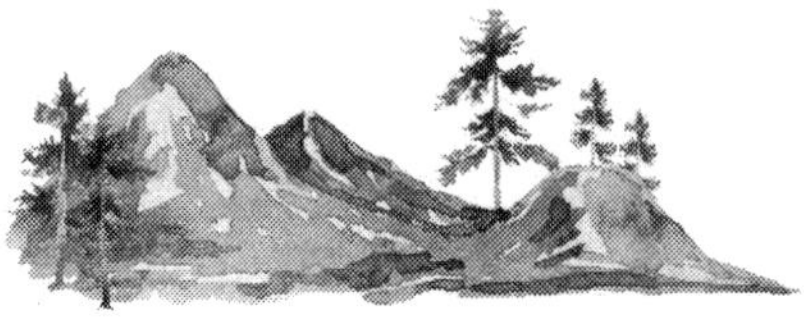

Date: ____________

Weather:

From: ____________

To: ____________

Route Taken: ____________

Beginning Mileage:

Ending Mileage:

Total Miles Traveled:

Campground Information

Name:

Address:

Phone:

Site # ________ $ ________ ☐ Day ☐ Week ☐ Month

☐ First Visit ☐ Return Visit ☐ Easy Access
☐ Site Level ☐ Back-in ☐ Pull-through
☐ 15 amp ☐ 30 amp ☐ 50 amp
☐ Water ☐ Sewer ☐ Shade ☐ Sun
☐ Paved ☐ Sand / Grass ☐ Gravel
☐ Picnic Table ☐ Fire ring ☐ Trees ☐ Lawn
☐ Patio ☐ Kid Friendly ☐ Pet Friendly
☐ Store ☐ Cafe ☐ Firewood
☐ Ice ☐ Security ☐ Quiet ☐ Noisy

Our Rating: ☆ ☆ ☆ ☆ ☆

GPS:

Altitude:

Cell Service / Carrier:

☐ Antenna Reception ☐ Satellite TV ☐ Cable TV
☐ WIFI Available ☐ Free ☐ Fee $ ________

Memberships:

Amenities:

Location	☺	😐	☹	Water Pressure	☺	😐	☹
Restrooms	☺	😐	☹	Laundry	☺	😐	☹
Pool	☺	😐	☹	Hot Tub	☺	😐	☹

Places Visited / Activities:

People Met / New Friends:

Food, Dining & Restaurants:

Highlights / Memorable Events:

Places To Go & Things To Do for Next Time:

Notes:

Date:

Weather:

From:

To:

Route Taken:

Beginning Mileage:

Ending Mileage:

Total Miles Traveled:

Campground Information

Name:

Address:

Phone:

Site # $ ☐ Day ☐ Week ☐ Month

☐ First Visit ☐ Return Visit ☐ Easy Access
☐ Site Level ☐ Back-in ☐ Pull-through
☐ 15 amp ☐ 30 amp ☐ 50 amp
☐ Water ☐ Sewer ☐ Shade ☐ Sun
☐ Paved ☐ Sand / Grass ☐ Gravel
☐ Picnic Table ☐ Fire ring ☐ Trees ☐ Lawn
☐ Patio ☐ Kid Friendly ☐ Pet Friendly
☐ Store ☐ Cafe ☐ Firewood
☐ Ice ☐ Security ☐ Quiet ☐ Noisy

Our Rating: ☆ ☆ ☆ ☆ ☆

GPS:

Altitude:

Cell Service / Carrier:

☐ Antenna Reception ☐ Satellite TV ☐ Cable TV
☐ WIFI Available ☐ Free ☐ Fee $

Memberships:

Amenities:

Location ☺ 😐 ☹ Water Pressure ☺ 😐 ☹
Restrooms ☺ 😐 ☹ Laundry ☺ 😐 ☹
Pool ☺ 😐 ☹ Hot Tub ☺ 😐 ☹

Places Visited / Activities:

People Met / New Friends:

Food, Dining & Restaurants:

Highlights / Memorable Events:

Places To Go & Things To Do for Next Time:

Notes:

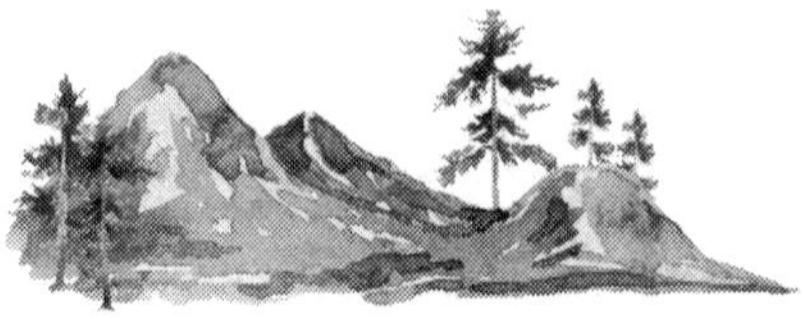

Date: ____________

Weather:

From: ____________

To: ____________

Route Taken: ____________

Beginning Mileage: ____________

Ending Mileage: ____________

Total Miles Traveled:

Campground Information

Name: ____________

Address: ____________

Phone: ____________

Site # ________ $ ________ ☐ Day ☐ Week ☐ Month

☐ First Visit	☐ Return Visit	☐ Easy Access	
☐ Site Level	☐ Back-in	☐ Pull-through	
☐ 15 amp	☐ 30 amp	☐ 50 amp	
☐ Water	☐ Sewer	☐ Shade	☐ Sun
☐ Paved	☐ Sand / Grass	☐ Gravel	
☐ Picnic Table	☐ Fire ring	☐ Trees	☐ Lawn
☐ Patio	☐ Kid Friendly	☐ Pet Friendly	
☐ Store	☐ Cafe	☐ Firewood	
☐ Ice	☐ Security	☐ Quiet	☐ Noisy

Our Rating: ☆ ☆ ☆ ☆ ☆

GPS: ____________

Altitude: ____________

Cell Service / Carrier: ____________

☐ Antenna Reception ☐ Satellite TV ☐ Cable TV

☐ WIFI Available ☐ Free ☐ Fee $ ________

Memberships: ____________

Amenities: ____________

Location	☺	😐	☹	Water Pressure	☺	😐	☹
Restrooms	☺	😐	☹	Laundry	☺	😐	☹
Pool	☺	😐	☹	Hot Tub	☺	😐	☹

Places Visited / Activities:

People Met / New Friends:

Food, Dining & Restaurants:

Highlights / Memorable Events:

Places To Go & Things To Do for Next Time:

NOTES:

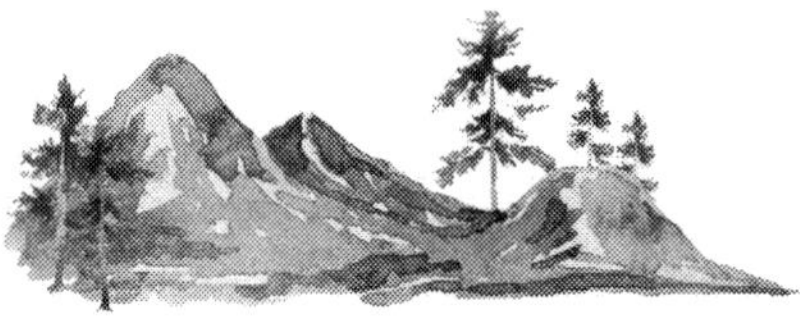

Date: ____________

Weather:

From: ____________

To: ____________

Route Taken: ____________

Beginning Mileage: ____________

Ending Mileage: ____________

Total Miles Traveled:

Campground Information

Name: ____________

Address: ____________

Phone: ____________

Site # ________ $ ________ ☐ Day ☐ Week ☐ Month

☐ First Visit	☐ Return Visit	☐ Easy Access	
☐ Site Level	☐ Back-in	☐ Pull-through	
☐ 15 amp	☐ 30 amp	☐ 50 amp	
☐ Water	☐ Sewer	☐ Shade	☐ Sun
☐ Paved	☐ Sand / Grass	☐ Gravel	
☐ Picnic Table	☐ Fire ring	☐ Trees	☐ Lawn
☐ Patio	☐ Kid Friendly	☐ Pet Friendly	
☐ Store	☐ Cafe	☐ Firewood	
☐ Ice	☐ Security	☐ Quiet	☐ Noisy

Our Rating: ☆ ☆ ☆ ☆ ☆

GPS: ____________

Altitude: ____________

Cell Service / Carrier: ____________

☐ Antenna Reception ☐ Satellite TV ☐ Cable TV

☐ WIFI Available ☐ Free ☐ Fee $ ________

Memberships: ____________

Amenities: ____________

Location	☺	😐	☹	Water Pressure	☺	😐	☹
Restrooms	☺	😐	☹	Laundry	☺	😐	☹
Pool	☺	😐	☹	Hot Tub	☺	😐	☹

Places Visited / Activities:

People Met / New Friends:

Food, Dining & Restaurants:

Highlights / Memorable Events:

Places To Go & Things To Do for Next Time:

Notes:

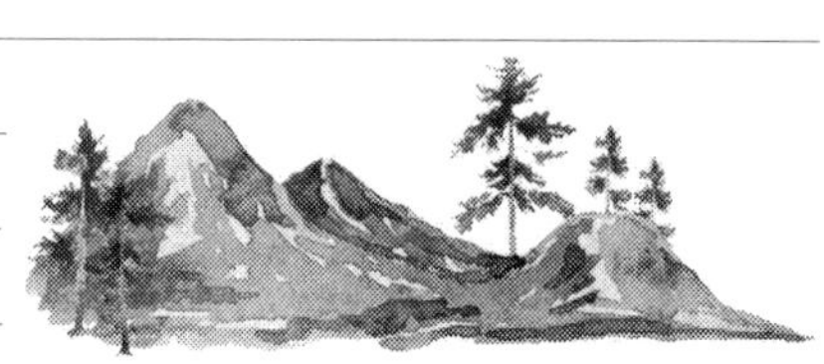

Date:

Weather:

From:

To:

Route Taken:

Beginning Mileage:

Ending Mileage:

Total Miles Traveled:

Campground Information

Name:

Address:

Phone:

Site # $ ☐ Day ☐ Week ☐ Month

☐ First Visit ☐ Return Visit ☐ Easy Access
☐ Site Level ☐ Back-in ☐ Pull-through
☐ 15 amp ☐ 30 amp ☐ 50 amp
☐ Water ☐ Sewer ☐ Shade ☐ Sun
☐ Paved ☐ Sand / Grass ☐ Gravel
☐ Picnic Table ☐ Fire ring ☐ Trees ☐ Lawn
☐ Patio ☐ Kid Friendly ☐ Pet Friendly
☐ Store ☐ Cafe ☐ Firewood
☐ Ice ☐ Security ☐ Quiet ☐ Noisy

Our Rating: ☆ ☆ ☆ ☆ ☆

GPS:

Altitude:

Cell Service / Carrier:

☐ Antenna Reception ☐ Satellite TV ☐ Cable TV
☐ WIFI Available ☐ Free ☐ Fee $

Memberships:

Amenities:

Location ☺ 😐 ☹ Water Pressure ☺ 😐 ☹
Restrooms ☺ 😐 ☹ Laundry ☺ 😐 ☹
Pool ☺ 😐 ☹ Hot Tub ☺ 😐 ☹

Places Visited / Activities:

People Met / New Friends:

Food, Dining & Restaurants:

Highlights / Memorable Events:

Places To Go & Things To Do for Next Time:

Notes:

Date: ______ From: ______ Beginning Mileage: ______

Weather: To: ______ Ending Mileage: ______

Route Taken: ______ Total Miles Traveled: ______

Campground Information

Name: ______ Our Rating: ☆ ☆ ☆ ☆ ☆

Address: ______ GPS: ______

Phone: ______ Altitude: ______

Site # ______ $ ______ ☐ Day ☐ Week ☐ Month

Cell Service / Carrier: ______

☐ First Visit	☐ Return Visit	☐ Easy Access	
☐ Site Level	☐ Back-in	☐ Pull-through	
☐ 15 amp	☐ 30 amp	☐ 50 amp	
☐ Water	☐ Sewer	☐ Shade	☐ Sun
☐ Paved	☐ Sand / Grass	☐ Gravel	
☐ Picnic Table	☐ Fire ring	☐ Trees	☐ Lawn
☐ Patio	☐ Kid Friendly	☐ Pet Friendly	
☐ Store	☐ Cafe	☐ Firewood	
☐ Ice	☐ Security	☐ Quiet	☐ Noisy

☐ Antenna Reception ☐ Satellite TV ☐ Cable TV

☐ WIFI Available ☐ Free ☐ Fee $ ______

Memberships: ______

Amenities: ______

Location	☺	😐	☹	Water Pressure	☺	😐	☹
Restrooms	☺	😐	☹	Laundry	☺	😐	☹
Pool	☺	😐	☹	Hot Tub	☺	😐	☹

Places Visited / Activities:

People Met / New Friends:

Food, Dining & Restaurants:

Highlights / Memorable Events:

Places To Go & Things To Do for Next Time:

Notes:

Date: ______	From: ______	Beginning Mileage: ______
Weather:	To: ______	Ending Mileage: ______
	Route Taken: ______	Total Miles Traveled:

Campground Information

Name: ______			
Address: ______			
Phone: ______			
Site # ______	$ ______	☐ Day ☐ Week	☐ Month
☐ First Visit	☐ Return Visit	☐ Easy Access	
☐ Site Level	☐ Back-in	☐ Pull-through	
☐ 15 amp	☐ 30 amp	☐ 50 amp	
☐ Water	☐ Sewer	☐ Shade	☐ Sun
☐ Paved	☐ Sand / Grass	☐ Gravel	
☐ Picnic Table	☐ Fire ring	☐ Trees	☐ Lawn
☐ Patio	☐ Kid Friendly	☐ Pet Friendly	
☐ Store	☐ Cafe	☐ Firewood	
☐ Ice	☐ Security	☐ Quiet	☐ Noisy

Our Rating: ☆ ☆ ☆ ☆ ☆

GPS: ______

Altitude: ______

Cell Service / Carrier: ______

☐ Antenna Reception ☐ Satellite TV ☐ Cable TV

☐ WIFI Available ☐ Free ☐ Fee $ ______

Memberships: ______

Amenities: ______

Location	☺ 😐 ☹	Water Pressure	☺ 😐 ☹
Restrooms	☺ 😐 ☹	Laundry	☺ 😐 ☹
Pool	☺ 😐 ☹	Hot Tub	☺ 😐 ☹

Places Visited / Activities:

People Met / New Friends:

Food, Dining & Restaurants:

Highlights / Memorable Events:

Places To Go & Things To Do for Next Time:

NOTES:

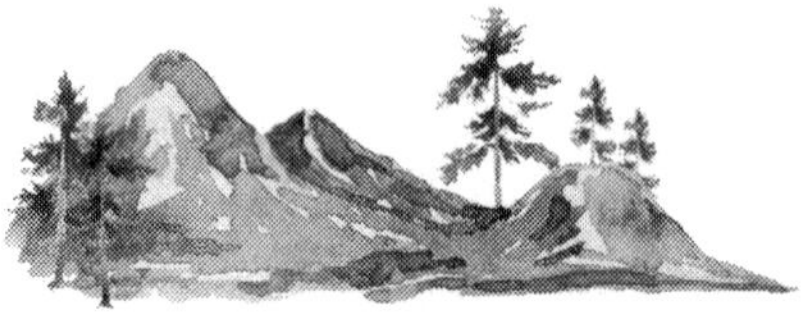

Date: ______ | From: ______ | Beginning Mileage: ______
Weather: | To: ______ | Ending Mileage: ______
Route Taken: ______ | Total Miles Traveled: ______

Campground Information

Name: ______
Address: ______
Phone: ______
Site # ______ $ ______ ☐ Day ☐ Week ☐ Month

☐ First Visit ☐ Return Visit ☐ Easy Access
☐ Site Level ☐ Back-in ☐ Pull-through
☐ 15 amp ☐ 30 amp ☐ 50 amp
☐ Water ☐ Sewer ☐ Shade ☐ Sun
☐ Paved ☐ Sand / Grass ☐ Gravel
☐ Picnic Table ☐ Fire ring ☐ Trees ☐ Lawn
☐ Patio ☐ Kid Friendly ☐ Pet Friendly
☐ Store ☐ Cafe ☐ Firewood
☐ Ice ☐ Security ☐ Quiet ☐ Noisy

Our Rating: ☆ ☆ ☆ ☆ ☆
GPS: ______
Altitude: ______
Cell Service / Carrier: ______
☐ Antenna Reception ☐ Satellite TV ☐ Cable TV
☐ WIFI Available ☐ Free ☐ Fee $ ______
Memberships: ______
Amenities: ______

Location	☺	😐	☹	Water Pressure	☺	😐	☹
Restrooms	☺	😐	☹	Laundry	☺	😐	☹
Pool	☺	😐	☹	Hot Tub	☺	😐	☹

Places Visited / Activities:

People Met / New Friends:

Food, Dining & Restaurants:

Highlights / Memorable Events:

Places To Go & Things To Do for Next Time:

Notes:

Date: ____ Weather:	From: ____ To: ____ Route Taken: ____	Beginning Mileage: ____ Ending Mileage: ____ Total Miles Traveled:

Campground Information

Name: ____
Address: ____
Phone: ____
Site # ____ $ ____ ☐ Day ☐ Week ☐ Month

☐ First Visit	☐ Return Visit	☐ Easy Access	
☐ Site Level	☐ Back-in	☐ Pull-through	
☐ 15 amp	☐ 30 amp	☐ 50 amp	
☐ Water	☐ Sewer	☐ Shade	☐ Sun
☐ Paved	☐ Sand / Grass	☐ Gravel	
☐ Picnic Table	☐ Fire ring	☐ Trees	☐ Lawn
☐ Patio	☐ Kid Friendly	☐ Pet Friendly	
☐ Store	☐ Cafe	☐ Firewood	
☐ Ice	☐ Security	☐ Quiet	☐ Noisy

Our Rating: ☆ ☆ ☆ ☆ ☆
GPS: ____
Altitude: ____
Cell Service / Carrier: ____

☐ Antenna Reception ☐ Satellite TV ☐ Cable TV
☐ WIFI Available ☐ Free ☐ Fee $ ____

Memberships: ____
Amenities: ____

Location	Water Pressure
Restrooms	Laundry
Pool	Hot Tub

Places Visited / Activities:

People Met / New Friends:

Food, Dining & Restaurants:

Highlights / Memorable Events:

Places To Go & Things To Do for Next Time:

Notes:

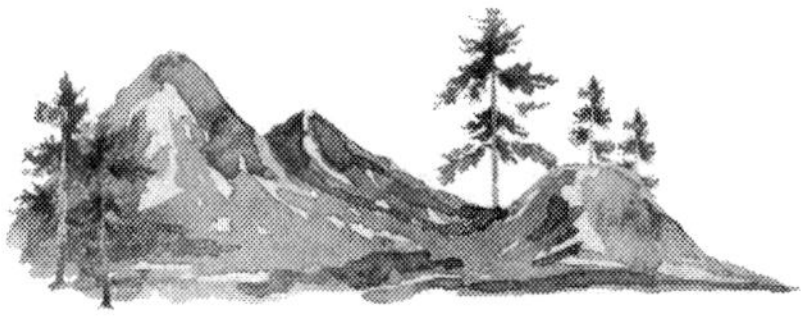

Date:

Weather:

From:

To:

Route Taken:

Beginning Mileage:

Ending Mileage:

Total Miles Traveled:

Campground Information

Name:

Address:

Phone:

Site # $ ☐ Day ☐ Week ☐ Month

☐ First Visit	☐ Return Visit	☐ Easy Access	
☐ Site Level	☐ Back-in	☐ Pull-through	
☐ 15 amp	☐ 30 amp	☐ 50 amp	
☐ Water	☐ Sewer	☐ Shade	☐ Sun
☐ Paved	☐ Sand / Grass	☐ Gravel	
☐ Picnic Table	☐ Fire ring	☐ Trees	☐ Lawn
☐ Patio	☐ Kid Friendly	☐ Pet Friendly	
☐ Store	☐ Cafe	☐ Firewood	
☐ Ice	☐ Security	☐ Quiet	☐ Noisy

Our Rating: ☆ ☆ ☆ ☆ ☆

GPS:

Altitude:

Cell Service / Carrier:

☐ Antenna Reception ☐ Satellite TV ☐ Cable TV

☐ WIFI Available ☐ Free ☐ Fee $

Memberships:

Amenities:

Location	☺	😐	☹	Water Pressure	☺	😐	☹
Restrooms	☺	😐	☹	Laundry	☺	😐	☹
Pool	☺	😐	☹	Hot Tub	☺	😐	☹

Places Visited / Activities:

People Met / New Friends:

Food, Dining & Restaurants:

Highlights / Memorable Events:

Places To Go & Things To Do for Next Time:

Notes:

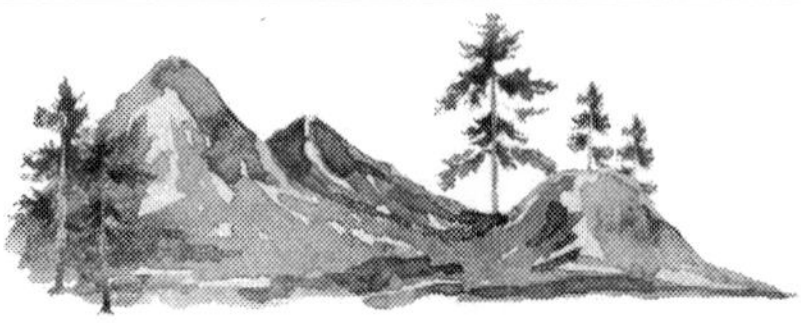

Date: ____________

Weather:

From: ____________

To: ____________

Route Taken: ____________

Beginning Mileage: ____________

Ending Mileage: ____________

Total Miles Traveled:

Campground Information

Name: ____________

Address: ____________

Phone: ____________

Site # ______ $ ______ ☐ Day ☐ Week ☐ Month

☐ First Visit	☐ Return Visit	☐ Easy Access	
☐ Site Level	☐ Back-in	☐ Pull-through	
☐ 15 amp	☐ 30 amp	☐ 50 amp	
☐ Water	☐ Sewer	☐ Shade	☐ Sun
☐ Paved	☐ Sand / Grass	☐ Gravel	
☐ Picnic Table	☐ Fire ring	☐ Trees	☐ Lawn
☐ Patio	☐ Kid Friendly	☐ Pet Friendly	
☐ Store	☐ Cafe	☐ Firewood	
☐ Ice	☐ Security	☐ Quiet	☐ Noisy

Our Rating: ☆ ☆ ☆ ☆ ☆

GPS: ____________

Altitude: ____________

Cell Service / Carrier: ____________

☐ Antenna Reception ☐ Satellite TV ☐ Cable TV

☐ WIFI Available ☐ Free ☐ Fee $ ______

Memberships: ____________

Amenities: ____________

Location	☺	😐	☹	Water Pressure	☺	😐	☹
Restrooms	☺	😐	☹	Laundry	☺	😐	☹
Pool	☺	😐	☹	Hot Tub	☺	😐	☹

Places Visited / Activities:

People Met / New Friends:

Food, Dining & Restaurants:

Highlights / Memorable Events:

Places To Go & Things To Do for Next Time:

NOTES:

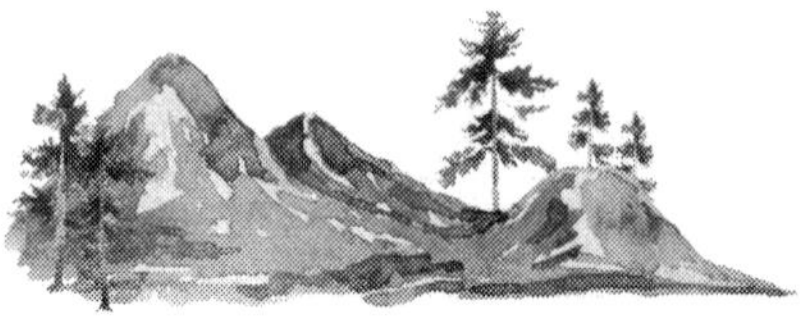

Date: ______	From: ______	Beginning Mileage: ______
Weather:	To: ______	Ending Mileage: ______
	Route Taken: ______	Total Miles Traveled:

Campground Information

Name: ______	Our Rating: ☆ ☆ ☆ ☆ ☆
Address: ______	GPS: ______
Phone: ______	Altitude: ______
Site # ______ $ ______ ☐ Day ☐ Week ☐ Month	Cell Service / Carrier: ______
☐ First Visit ☐ Return Visit ☐ Easy Access	☐ Antenna Reception ☐ Satellite TV ☐ Cable TV
☐ Site Level ☐ Back-in ☐ Pull-through	☐ WIFI Available ☐ Free ☐ Fee $ ______
☐ 15 amp ☐ 30 amp ☐ 50 amp	Memberships: ______
☐ Water ☐ Sewer ☐ Shade ☐ Sun	Amenities: ______
☐ Paved ☐ Sand / Grass ☐ Gravel	
☐ Picnic Table ☐ Fire ring ☐ Trees ☐ Lawn	Location ☺ 😐 ☹ Water Pressure ☺ 😐 ☹
☐ Patio ☐ Kid Friendly ☐ Pet Friendly	Restrooms ☺ 😐 ☹ Laundry ☺ 😐 ☹
☐ Store ☐ Cafe ☐ Firewood	Pool ☺ 😐 ☹ Hot Tub ☺ 😐 ☹
☐ Ice ☐ Security ☐ Quiet ☐ Noisy	

Places Visited / Activities:

People Met / New Friends:

Food, Dining & Restaurants:

Highlights / Memorable Events:

Places To Go & Things To Do for Next Time:

Notes:

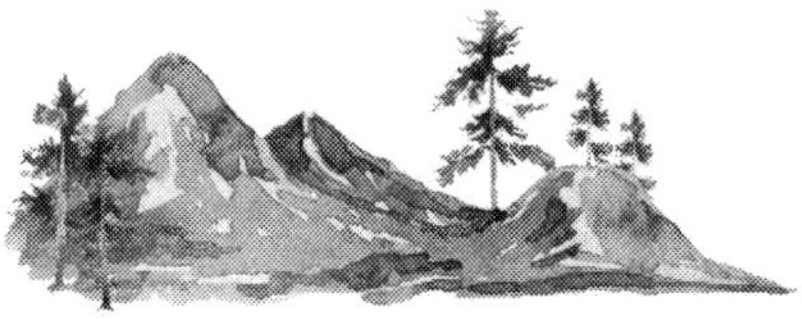

Date:

Weather:

From:

To:

Route Taken:

Beginning Mileage:

Ending Mileage:

Total Miles Traveled:

Campground Information

Name:

Address:

Phone:

Site # $ ☐ Day ☐ Week ☐ Month

☐ First Visit ☐ Return Visit ☐ Easy Access
☐ Site Level ☐ Back-in ☐ Pull-through
☐ 15 amp ☐ 30 amp ☐ 50 amp
☐ Water ☐ Sewer ☐ Shade ☐ Sun
☐ Paved ☐ Sand / Grass ☐ Gravel
☐ Picnic Table ☐ Fire ring ☐ Trees ☐ Lawn
☐ Patio ☐ Kid Friendly ☐ Pet Friendly
☐ Store ☐ Cafe ☐ Firewood
☐ Ice ☐ Security ☐ Quiet ☐ Noisy

Our Rating: ☆ ☆ ☆ ☆ ☆

GPS:

Altitude:

Cell Service / Carrier:

☐ Antenna Reception ☐ Satellite TV ☐ Cable TV
☐ WIFI Available ☐ Free ☐ Fee $

Memberships:

Amenities:

Location ☺ 😐 ☹ Water Pressure ☺ 😐 ☹
Restrooms ☺ 😐 ☹ Laundry ☺ 😐 ☹
Pool ☺ 😐 ☹ Hot Tub ☺ 😐 ☹

Places Visited / Activities:

People Met / New Friends:

Food, Dining & Restaurants:

Highlights / Memorable Events:

Places To Go & Things To Do for Next Time:

NOTES:

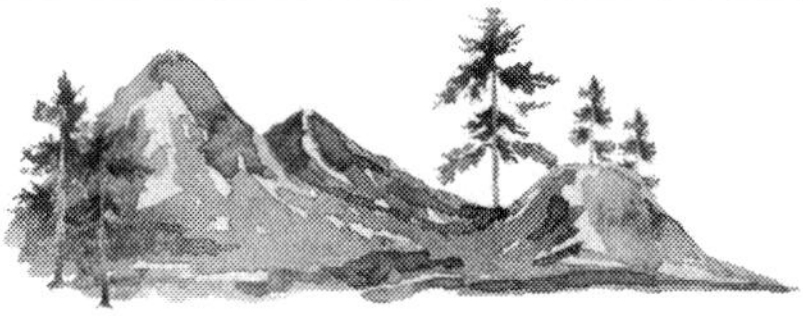

Date:

Weather:

From:

To:

Route Taken:

Beginning Mileage:

Ending Mileage:

Total Miles Traveled:

Campground Information

Name:

Address:

Phone:

Site # $ ☐ Day ☐ Week ☐ Month

☐ First Visit ☐ Return Visit ☐ Easy Access
☐ Site Level ☐ Back-in ☐ Pull-through
☐ 15 amp ☐ 30 amp ☐ 50 amp
☐ Water ☐ Sewer ☐ Shade ☐ Sun
☐ Paved ☐ Sand / Grass ☐ Gravel
☐ Picnic Table ☐ Fire ring ☐ Trees ☐ Lawn
☐ Patio ☐ Kid Friendly ☐ Pet Friendly
☐ Store ☐ Cafe ☐ Firewood
☐ Ice ☐ Security ☐ Quiet ☐ Noisy

Our Rating: ☆ ☆ ☆ ☆ ☆

GPS:

Altitude:

Cell Service / Carrier:

☐ Antenna Reception ☐ Satellite TV ☐ Cable TV
☐ WIFI Available ☐ Free ☐ Fee $

Memberships:

Amenities:

Location ☺ 😐 ☹ Water Pressure ☺ 😐 ☹
Restrooms ☺ 😐 ☹ Laundry ☺ 😐 ☹
Pool ☺ 😐 ☹ Hot Tub ☺ 😐 ☹

Places Visited / Activities:

People Met / New Friends:

Food, Dining & Restaurants:

Highlights / Memorable Events:

Places To Go & Things To Do for Next Time:

Notes:

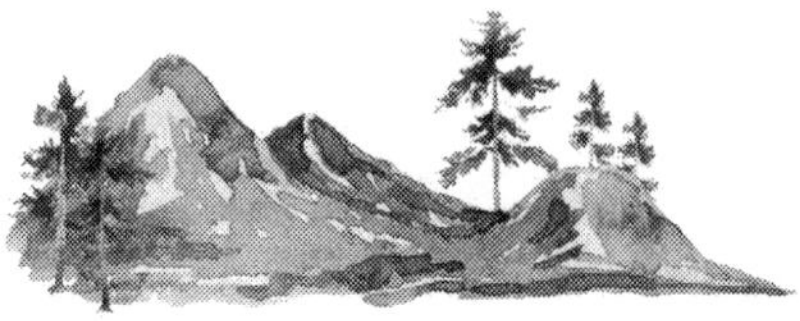

Date: ______	From: ______	Beginning Mileage: ______
Weather:	To: ______	Ending Mileage: ______
	Route Taken: ______	Total Miles Traveled:

Campground Information

Name: ______			
Address: ______			
Phone: ______			
Site # ______	$ ______	☐ Day ☐ Week ☐ Month	
☐ First Visit	☐ Return Visit	☐ Easy Access	
☐ Site Level	☐ Back-in	☐ Pull-through	
☐ 15 amp	☐ 30 amp	☐ 50 amp	
☐ Water	☐ Sewer	☐ Shade	☐ Sun
☐ Paved	☐ Sand / Grass	☐ Gravel	
☐ Picnic Table	☐ Fire ring	☐ Trees	☐ Lawn
☐ Patio	☐ Kid Friendly	☐ Pet Friendly	
☐ Store	☐ Cafe	☐ Firewood	
☐ Ice	☐ Security	☐ Quiet	☐ Noisy

Our Rating: ☆ ☆ ☆ ☆ ☆

GPS: ______

Altitude: ______

Cell Service / Carrier: ______

☐ Antenna Reception ☐ Satellite TV ☐ Cable TV

☐ WIFI Available ☐ Free ☐ Fee $ ______

Memberships: ______

Amenities: ______

Location	☺	😐	☹	Water Pressure	☺	😐	☹
Restrooms	☺	😐	☹	Laundry	☺	😐	☹
Pool	☺	😐	☹	Hot Tub	☺	😐	☹

Places Visited / Activities:

People Met / New Friends:

Food, Dining & Restaurants:

Highlights / Memorable Events:

Places To Go & Things To Do for Next Time:

NOTES:

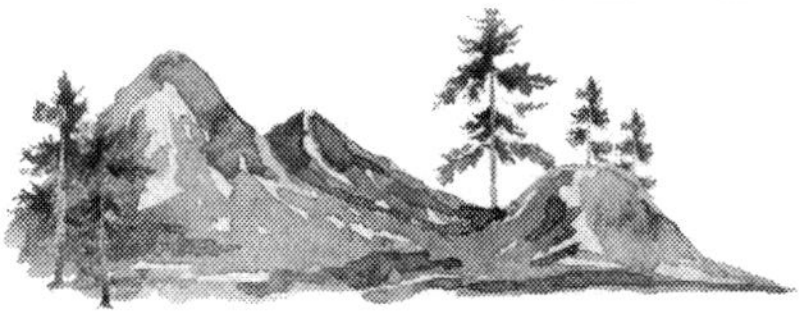

Date: ______

Weather:

From: ______

To: ______

Route Taken: ______

Beginning Mileage: ______

Ending Mileage: ______

Total Miles Traveled:

Campground Information

Name: ______

Address: ______

Phone: ______

Site # ______ $ ______ ☐ Day ☐ Week ☐ Month

☐ First Visit	☐ Return Visit	☐ Easy Access	
☐ Site Level	☐ Back-in	☐ Pull-through	
☐ 15 amp	☐ 30 amp	☐ 50 amp	
☐ Water	☐ Sewer	☐ Shade	☐ Sun
☐ Paved	☐ Sand / Grass	☐ Gravel	
☐ Picnic Table	☐ Fire ring	☐ Trees	☐ Lawn
☐ Patio	☐ Kid Friendly	☐ Pet Friendly	
☐ Store	☐ Cafe	☐ Firewood	
☐ Ice	☐ Security	☐ Quiet	☐ Noisy

Our Rating: ☆ ☆ ☆ ☆ ☆

GPS: ______

Altitude: ______

Cell Service / Carrier: ______

☐ Antenna Reception ☐ Satellite TV ☐ Cable TV

☐ WIFI Available ☐ Free ☐ Fee $ ______

Memberships: ______

Amenities: ______

Location	☺	😐	☹	Water Pressure	☺	😐	☹
Restrooms	☺	😐	☹	Laundry	☺	😐	☹
Pool	☺	😐	☹	Hot Tub	☺	😐	☹

Places Visited / Activities: ______

People Met / New Friends: ______

Food, Dining & Restaurants: ______

Highlights / Memorable Events: ______

Places To Go & Things To Do for Next Time: ______

Notes:

Date:

Weather:

From:

To:

Route Taken:

Beginning Mileage:

Ending Mileage:

Total Miles Traveled:

Campground Information

Name:

Address:

Phone:

Site # $ ☐ Day ☐ Week ☐ Month

☐ First Visit ☐ Return Visit ☐ Easy Access
☐ Site Level ☐ Back-in ☐ Pull-through
☐ 15 amp ☐ 30 amp ☐ 50 amp
☐ Water ☐ Sewer ☐ Shade ☐ Sun
☐ Paved ☐ Sand / Grass ☐ Gravel
☐ Picnic Table ☐ Fire ring ☐ Trees ☐ Lawn
☐ Patio ☐ Kid Friendly ☐ Pet Friendly
☐ Store ☐ Cafe ☐ Firewood
☐ Ice ☐ Security ☐ Quiet ☐ Noisy

Our Rating: ☆ ☆ ☆ ☆ ☆

GPS:

Altitude:

Cell Service / Carrier:

☐ Antenna Reception ☐ Satellite TV ☐ Cable TV
☐ WIFI Available ☐ Free ☐ Fee $

Memberships:

Amenities:

Location ☺ 😐 ☹ Water Pressure ☺ 😐 ☹
Restrooms ☺ 😐 ☹ Laundry ☺ 😐 ☹
Pool ☺ 😐 ☹ Hot Tub ☺ 😐 ☹

Places Visited / Activities:

People Met / New Friends:

Food, Dining & Restaurants:

Highlights / Memorable Events:

Places To Go & Things To Do for Next Time:

NOTES:

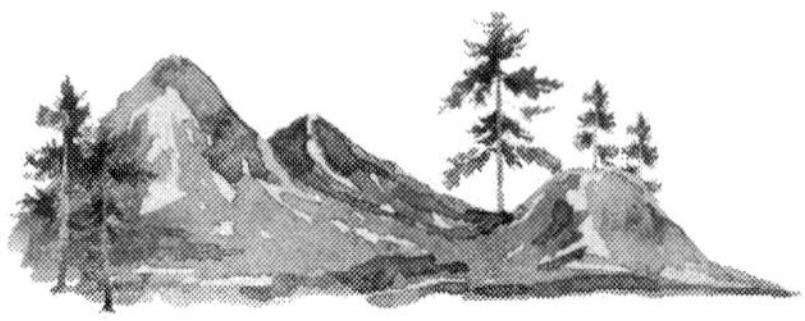

Date: ______

Weather:

From: ______

To: ______

Route Taken: ______

Beginning Mileage: ______

Ending Mileage: ______

Total Miles Traveled:

Campground Information

Name: ______

Address: ______

Phone: ______

Site # ______ $ ______ ☐ Day ☐ Week ☐ Month

☐ First Visit ☐ Return Visit ☐ Easy Access
☐ Site Level ☐ Back-in ☐ Pull-through
☐ 15 amp ☐ 30 amp ☐ 50 amp
☐ Water ☐ Sewer ☐ Shade ☐ Sun
☐ Paved ☐ Sand / Grass ☐ Gravel
☐ Picnic Table ☐ Fire ring ☐ Trees ☐ Lawn
☐ Patio ☐ Kid Friendly ☐ Pet Friendly
☐ Store ☐ Cafe ☐ Firewood
☐ Ice ☐ Security ☐ Quiet ☐ Noisy

Our Rating: ☆ ☆ ☆ ☆ ☆

GPS: ______

Altitude: ______

Cell Service / Carrier: ______

☐ Antenna Reception ☐ Satellite TV ☐ Cable TV
☐ WIFI Available ☐ Free ☐ Fee $ ______

Memberships: ______

Amenities: ______

Location ☺ 😐 ☹ Water Pressure ☺ 😐 ☹
Restrooms ☺ 😐 ☹ Laundry ☺ 😐 ☹
Pool ☺ 😐 ☹ Hot Tub ☺ 😐 ☹

Places Visited / Activities:

People Met / New Friends:

Food, Dining & Restaurants:

Highlights / Memorable Events:

Places To Go & Things To Do for Next Time:

Notes:

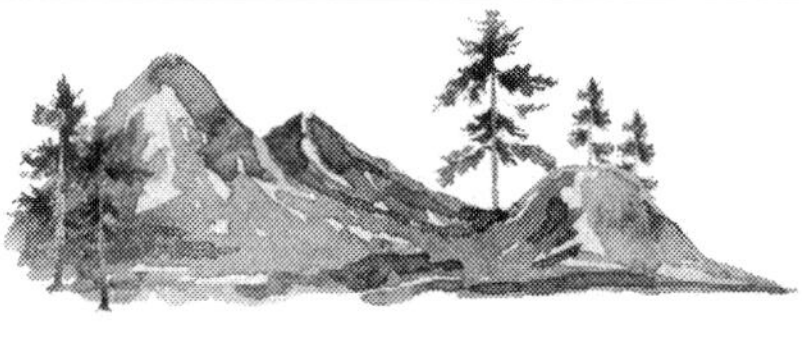

Date: ______

Weather:

From: ______

To: ______

Route Taken: ______

Beginning Mileage: ______

Ending Mileage: ______

Total Miles Traveled:

Campground Information

Name: ______

Address: ______

Phone: ______

Site # ______ $ ______ ☐ Day ☐ Week ☐ Month

☐ First Visit	☐ Return Visit	☐ Easy Access	
☐ Site Level	☐ Back-in	☐ Pull-through	
☐ 15 amp	☐ 30 amp	☐ 50 amp	
☐ Water	☐ Sewer	☐ Shade	☐ Sun
☐ Paved	☐ Sand / Grass	☐ Gravel	
☐ Picnic Table	☐ Fire ring	☐ Trees	☐ Lawn
☐ Patio	☐ Kid Friendly	☐ Pet Friendly	
☐ Store	☐ Cafe	☐ Firewood	
☐ Ice	☐ Security	☐ Quiet	☐ Noisy

Our Rating: ☆ ☆ ☆ ☆ ☆

GPS: ______

Altitude: ______

Cell Service / Carrier: ______

☐ Antenna Reception ☐ Satellite TV ☐ Cable TV

☐ WIFI Available ☐ Free ☐ Fee $ ______

Memberships: ______

Amenities: ______

Location	☺	😐	☹	Water Pressure	☺	😐	☹
Restrooms	☺	😐	☹	Laundry	☺	😐	☹
Pool	☺	😐	☹	Hot Tub	☺	😐	☹

Places Visited / Activities:

People Met / New Friends:

Food, Dining & Restaurants:

Highlights / Memorable Events:

Places To Go & Things To Do for Next Time:

Notes:

Date: ____

Weather:

From: ____

To: ____

Route Taken: ____

Beginning Mileage: ____

Ending Mileage: ____

Total Miles Traveled:

Campground Information

Name: ____

Address: ____

Phone: ____

Site # ____ $ ____ ☐ Day ☐ Week ☐ Month

☐ First Visit	☐ Return Visit	☐ Easy Access	
☐ Site Level	☐ Back-in	☐ Pull-through	
☐ 15 amp	☐ 30 amp	☐ 50 amp	
☐ Water	☐ Sewer	☐ Shade	☐ Sun
☐ Paved	☐ Sand / Grass	☐ Gravel	
☐ Picnic Table	☐ Fire ring	☐ Trees	☐ Lawn
☐ Patio	☐ Kid Friendly	☐ Pet Friendly	
☐ Store	☐ Cafe	☐ Firewood	
☐ Ice	☐ Security	☐ Quiet	☐ Noisy

Our Rating: ☆ ☆ ☆ ☆ ☆

GPS: ____

Altitude: ____

Cell Service / Carrier: ____

☐ Antenna Reception ☐ Satellite TV ☐ Cable TV

☐ WIFI Available ☐ Free ☐ Fee $ ____

Memberships: ____

Amenities: ____

Location	☺	😐	☹	Water Pressure	☺	😐	☹
Restrooms	☺	😐	☹	Laundry	☺	😐	☹
Pool	☺	😐	☹	Hot Tub	☺	😐	☹

Places Visited / Activities:

People Met / New Friends:

Food, Dining & Restaurants:

Highlights / Memorable Events:

Places To Go & Things To Do for Next Time:

Notes:

Date:	From:	Beginning Mileage:
Weather:	To:	Ending Mileage:
	Route Taken:	Total Miles Traveled:

Campground Information

Name:			
Address:			
Phone:			
Site #	$	☐ Day ☐ Week	☐ Month
☐ First Visit	☐ Return Visit	☐ Easy Access	
☐ Site Level	☐ Back-in	☐ Pull-through	
☐ 15 amp	☐ 30 amp	☐ 50 amp	
☐ Water	☐ Sewer	☐ Shade	☐ Sun
☐ Paved	☐ Sand / Grass	☐ Gravel	
☐ Picnic Table	☐ Fire ring	☐ Trees	☐ Lawn
☐ Patio	☐ Kid Friendly	☐ Pet Friendly	
☐ Store	☐ Cafe	☐ Firewood	
☐ Ice	☐ Security	☐ Quiet	☐ Noisy

Our Rating: ☆ ☆ ☆ ☆ ☆

GPS:

Altitude:

Cell Service / Carrier:

☐ Antenna Reception ☐ Satellite TV ☐ Cable TV

☐ WIFI Available ☐ Free ☐ Fee $

Memberships:

Amenities:

Location	☺	😐	☹	Water Pressure	☺	😐	☹
Restrooms	☺	😐	☹	Laundry	☺	😐	☹
Pool	☺	😐	☹	Hot Tub	☺	😐	☹

Places Visited / Activities:

People Met / New Friends:

Food, Dining & Restaurants:

Highlights / Memorable Events:

Places To Go & Things To Do for Next Time:

Notes:

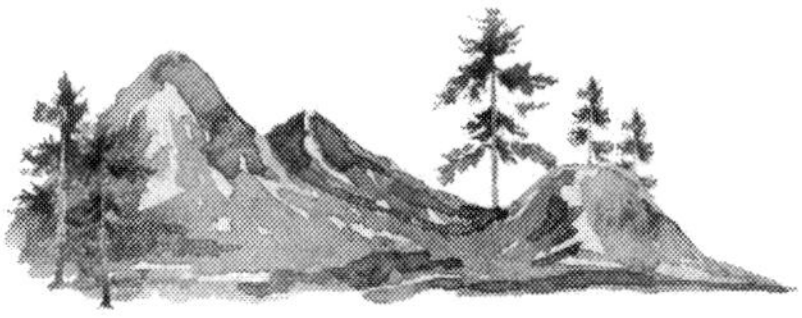

Date: ______ From: ______ Beginning Mileage: ______

Weather: To: ______ Ending Mileage: ______

Route Taken: ______ Total Miles Traveled: ______

Campground Information

Name: ______	Our Rating: ☆ ☆ ☆ ☆ ☆
Address: ______	GPS: ______
Phone: ______	Altitude: ______
Site # ______ $ ______ ☐ Day ☐ Week ☐ Month	Cell Service / Carrier: ______

☐ First Visit	☐ Return Visit	☐ Easy Access	
☐ Site Level	☐ Back-in	☐ Pull-through	
☐ 15 amp	☐ 30 amp	☐ 50 amp	
☐ Water	☐ Sewer	☐ Shade	☐ Sun
☐ Paved	☐ Sand / Grass	☐ Gravel	
☐ Picnic Table	☐ Fire ring	☐ Trees	☐ Lawn
☐ Patio	☐ Kid Friendly	☐ Pet Friendly	
☐ Store	☐ Cafe	☐ Firewood	
☐ Ice	☐ Security	☐ Quiet	☐ Noisy

☐ Antenna Reception ☐ Satellite TV ☐ Cable TV

☐ WIFI Available ☐ Free ☐ Fee $ ______

Memberships: ______

Amenities: ______

Location ☺ 😐 ☹		Water Pressure ☺ 😐 ☹
Restrooms ☺ 😐 ☹		Laundry ☺ 😐 ☹
Pool ☺ 😐 ☹		Hot Tub ☺ 😐 ☹

Places Visited / Activities:

People Met / New Friends:

Food, Dining & Restaurants:

Highlights / Memorable Events:

Places To Go & Things To Do for Next Time:

NOTES:

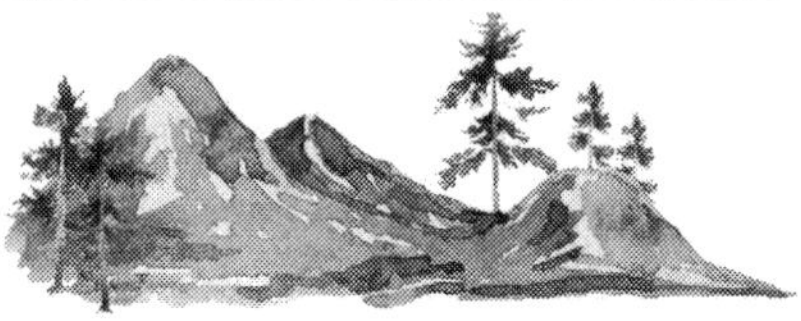

Date:	From:	Beginning Mileage:
Weather:	To:	Ending Mileage:
	Route Taken:	Total Miles Traveled:

Campground Information

Name:				
Address:				
Phone:				
Site #	$	Day	Week	Month
First Visit	Return Visit	Easy Access		
Site Level	Back-in	Pull-through		
15 amp	30 amp	50 amp		
Water	Sewer	Shade	Sun	
Paved	Sand / Grass	Gravel		
Picnic Table	Fire ring	Trees	Lawn	
Patio	Kid Friendly	Pet Friendly		
Store	Cafe	Firewood		
Ice	Security	Quiet	Noisy	

Our Rating:

GPS:

Altitude:

Cell Service / Carrier:

Antenna Reception	Satellite TV	Cable TV
WIFI Available	Free	Fee $

Memberships:

Amenities:

Location	Water Pressure
Restrooms	Laundry
Pool	Hot Tub

Places Visited / Activities:

People Met / New Friends:

Food, Dining & Restaurants:

Highlights / Memorable Events:

Places To Go & Things To Do for Next Time:

Notes:

Date: ____________

Weather:

From: ____________

To: ____________

Route Taken: ____________

Beginning Mileage:

Ending Mileage:

Total Miles Traveled:

Campground Information

Name:

Address:

Phone:

Site # ______ $ ______ ☐ Day ☐ Week ☐ Month

☐ First Visit	☐ Return Visit	☐ Easy Access	
☐ Site Level	☐ Back-in	☐ Pull-through	
☐ 15 amp	☐ 30 amp	☐ 50 amp	
☐ Water	☐ Sewer	☐ Shade	☐ Sun
☐ Paved	☐ Sand / Grass	☐ Gravel	
☐ Picnic Table	☐ Fire ring	☐ Trees	☐ Lawn
☐ Patio	☐ Kid Friendly	☐ Pet Friendly	
☐ Store	☐ Cafe	☐ Firewood	
☐ Ice	☐ Security	☐ Quiet	☐ Noisy

Our Rating: ☆ ☆ ☆ ☆ ☆

GPS:

Altitude:

Cell Service / Carrier:

☐ Antenna Reception ☐ Satellite TV ☐ Cable TV

☐ WIFI Available ☐ Free ☐ Fee $ ______

Memberships:

Amenities:

Location	☺	😐	☹	Water Pressure	☺	😐	☹
Restrooms	☺	😐	☹	Laundry	☺	😐	☹
Pool	☺	😐	☹	Hot Tub	☺	😐	☹

Places Visited / Activities:

People Met / New Friends:

Food, Dining & Restaurants:

Highlights / Memorable Events:

Places To Go & Things To Do for Next Time:

Notes:

Date:

Weather:

From:

To:

Route Taken:

Beginning Mileage:

Ending Mileage:

Total Miles Traveled:

Campground Information

Name:

Address:

Phone:

Site # $ ☐ Day ☐ Week ☐ Month

☐ First Visit ☐ Return Visit ☐ Easy Access
☐ Site Level ☐ Back-in ☐ Pull-through
☐ 15 amp ☐ 30 amp ☐ 50 amp
☐ Water ☐ Sewer ☐ Shade ☐ Sun
☐ Paved ☐ Sand / Grass ☐ Gravel
☐ Picnic Table ☐ Fire ring ☐ Trees ☐ Lawn
☐ Patio ☐ Kid Friendly ☐ Pet Friendly
☐ Store ☐ Cafe ☐ Firewood
☐ Ice ☐ Security ☐ Quiet ☐ Noisy

Our Rating: ☆ ☆ ☆ ☆ ☆

GPS:

Altitude:

Cell Service / Carrier:

☐ Antenna Reception ☐ Satellite TV ☐ Cable TV
☐ WIFI Available ☐ Free ☐ Fee $

Memberships:

Amenities:

Location	☺	😐	☹	Water Pressure	☺	😐	☹
Restrooms	☺	😐	☹	Laundry	☺	😐	☹
Pool	☺	😐	☹	Hot Tub	☺	😐	☹

Places Visited / Activities:

People Met / New Friends:

Food, Dining & Restaurants:

Highlights / Memorable Events:

Places To Go & Things To Do for Next Time:

Notes:

Date: ______	From: ______	Beginning Mileage: ______
Weather:	To: ______	Ending Mileage: ______
	Route Taken: ______	Total Miles Traveled:

Campground Information

Name: ______		Our Rating: ☆ ☆ ☆ ☆ ☆	
Address: ______		GPS: ______	
Phone: ______		Altitude: ______	
Site # ______	$ ______	☐ Day ☐ Week ☐ Month	Cell Service / Carrier: ______

☐ First Visit	☐ Return Visit	☐ Easy Access	
☐ Site Level	☐ Back-in	☐ Pull-through	
☐ 15 amp	☐ 30 amp	☐ 50 amp	
☐ Water	☐ Sewer	☐ Shade	☐ Sun
☐ Paved	☐ Sand / Grass	☐ Gravel	
☐ Picnic Table	☐ Fire ring	☐ Trees	☐ Lawn
☐ Patio	☐ Kid Friendly	☐ Pet Friendly	
☐ Store	☐ Cafe	☐ Firewood	
☐ Ice	☐ Security	☐ Quiet	☐ Noisy

☐ Antenna Reception ☐ Satellite TV ☐ Cable TV

☐ WIFI Available ☐ Free ☐ Fee $ ______

Memberships: ______

Amenities: ______

Location	☺	😐	☹	Water Pressure	☺	😐	☹
Restrooms	☺	😐	☹	Laundry	☺	😐	☹
Pool	☺	😐	☹	Hot Tub	☺	😐	☹

Places Visited / Activities: ______

People Met / New Friends: ______

Food, Dining & Restaurants: ______

Highlights / Memorable Events: ______

Places To Go & Things To Do for Next Time: ______

NOTES:

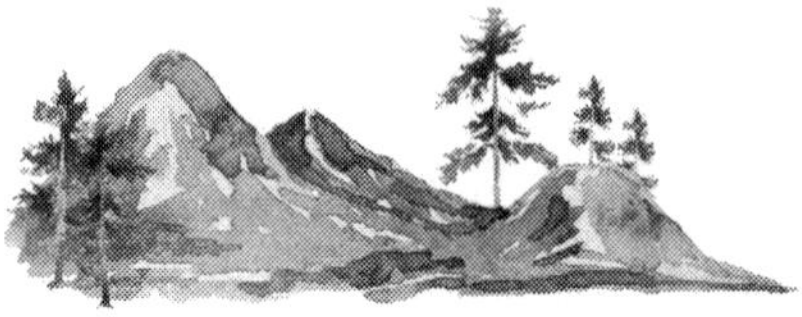

Date:	From:	Beginning Mileage:
Weather:	To:	Ending Mileage:
	Route Taken:	Total Miles Traveled:

Campground Information

Name:

Address:

Phone:

Site # $ ☐ Day ☐ Week ☐ Month

☐ First Visit	☐ Return Visit	☐ Easy Access	
☐ Site Level	☐ Back-in	☐ Pull-through	
☐ 15 amp	☐ 30 amp	☐ 50 amp	
☐ Water	☐ Sewer	☐ Shade	☐ Sun
☐ Paved	☐ Sand / Grass	☐ Gravel	
☐ Picnic Table	☐ Fire ring	☐ Trees	☐ Lawn
☐ Patio	☐ Kid Friendly	☐ Pet Friendly	
☐ Store	☐ Cafe	☐ Firewood	
☐ Ice	☐ Security	☐ Quiet	☐ Noisy

Our Rating: ☆ ☆ ☆ ☆ ☆

GPS:

Altitude:

Cell Service / Carrier:

☐ Antenna Reception ☐ Satellite TV ☐ Cable TV

☐ WIFI Available ☐ Free ☐ Fee $

Memberships:

Amenities:

Location	☺	😐	☹	Water Pressure	☺	😐	☹
Restrooms	☺	😐	☹	Laundry	☺	😐	☹
Pool	☺	😐	☹	Hot Tub	☺	😐	☹

Places Visited / Activities:

People Met / New Friends:

Food, Dining & Restaurants:

Highlights / Memorable Events:

Places To Go & Things To Do for Next Time:

Notes:

Date:

Weather:

From:

To:

Route Taken:

Beginning Mileage:

Ending Mileage:

Total Miles Traveled:

Campground Information

Name:

Address:

Phone:

Site # $ ☐ Day ☐ Week ☐ Month

☐ First Visit	☐ Return Visit	☐ Easy Access	
☐ Site Level	☐ Back-in	☐ Pull-through	
☐ 15 amp	☐ 30 amp	☐ 50 amp	
☐ Water	☐ Sewer	☐ Shade	☐ Sun
☐ Paved	☐ Sand / Grass	☐ Gravel	
☐ Picnic Table	☐ Fire ring	☐ Trees	☐ Lawn
☐ Patio	☐ Kid Friendly	☐ Pet Friendly	
☐ Store	☐ Cafe	☐ Firewood	
☐ Ice	☐ Security	☐ Quiet	☐ Noisy

Our Rating: ☆ ☆ ☆ ☆ ☆

GPS:

Altitude:

Cell Service / Carrier:

☐ Antenna Reception ☐ Satellite TV ☐ Cable TV

☐ WIFI Available ☐ Free ☐ Fee $

Memberships:

Amenities:

Location	☺	😐	☹	Water Pressure	☺	😐	☹
Restrooms	☺	😐	☹	Laundry	☺	😐	☹
Pool	☺	😐	☹	Hot Tub	☺	😐	☹

Places Visited / Activities:

People Met / New Friends:

Food, Dining & Restaurants:

Highlights / Memorable Events:

Places To Go & Things To Do for Next Time:

Notes:

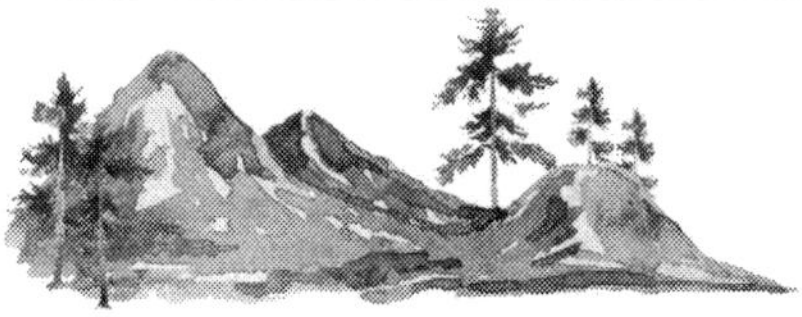

Date:	From:	Beginning Mileage:
Weather:	To:	Ending Mileage:
	Route Taken:	Total Miles Traveled:

Campground Information

Name:			
Address:			
Phone:			
Site #	$	☐ Day ☐ Week	☐ Month
☐ First Visit	☐ Return Visit	☐ Easy Access	
☐ Site Level	☐ Back-in	☐ Pull-through	
☐ 15 amp	☐ 30 amp	☐ 50 amp	
☐ Water	☐ Sewer	☐ Shade	☐ Sun
☐ Paved	☐ Sand / Grass	☐ Gravel	
☐ Picnic Table	☐ Fire ring	☐ Trees	☐ Lawn
☐ Patio	☐ Kid Friendly	☐ Pet Friendly	
☐ Store	☐ Cafe	☐ Firewood	
☐ Ice	☐ Security	☐ Quiet	☐ Noisy

Our Rating: ☆ ☆ ☆ ☆ ☆

GPS:

Altitude:

Cell Service / Carrier:

☐ Antenna Reception ☐ Satellite TV ☐ Cable TV

☐ WIFI Available ☐ Free ☐ Fee $

Memberships:

Amenities:

Location	☺	😐	☹	Water Pressure	☺	😐	☹
Restrooms	☺	😐	☹	Laundry	☺	😐	☹
Pool	☺	😐	☹	Hot Tub	☺	😐	☹

Places Visited / Activities:

People Met / New Friends:

Food, Dining & Restaurants:

Highlights / Memorable Events:

Places To Go & Things To Do for Next Time:

Notes:

Date: ____________

Weather:

From: ____________

To: ____________

Route Taken: ____________

Beginning Mileage:

Ending Mileage:

Total Miles Traveled:

Campground Information

Name: ____________

Address: ____________

Phone: ____________

Site # ________ $ ________ ☐ Day ☐ Week ☐ Month

☐ First Visit	☐ Return Visit	☐ Easy Access	
☐ Site Level	☐ Back-in	☐ Pull-through	
☐ 15 amp	☐ 30 amp	☐ 50 amp	
☐ Water	☐ Sewer	☐ Shade	☐ Sun
☐ Paved	☐ Sand / Grass	☐ Gravel	
☐ Picnic Table	☐ Fire ring	☐ Trees	☐ Lawn
☐ Patio	☐ Kid Friendly	☐ Pet Friendly	
☐ Store	☐ Cafe	☐ Firewood	
☐ Ice	☐ Security	☐ Quiet	☐ Noisy

Our Rating: ☆ ☆ ☆ ☆ ☆

GPS: ____________

Altitude: ____________

Cell Service / Carrier: ____________

☐ Antenna Reception ☐ Satellite TV ☐ Cable TV

☐ WIFI Available ☐ Free ☐ Fee $ ________

Memberships: ____________

Amenities: ____________

Location	☺	😐	☹	Water Pressure	☺	😐	☹
Restrooms	☺	😐	☹	Laundry	☺	😐	☹
Pool	☺	😐	☹	Hot Tub	☺	😐	☹

Places Visited / Activities:

People Met / New Friends:

Food, Dining & Restaurants:

Highlights / Memorable Events:

Places To Go & Things To Do for Next Time:

Notes:

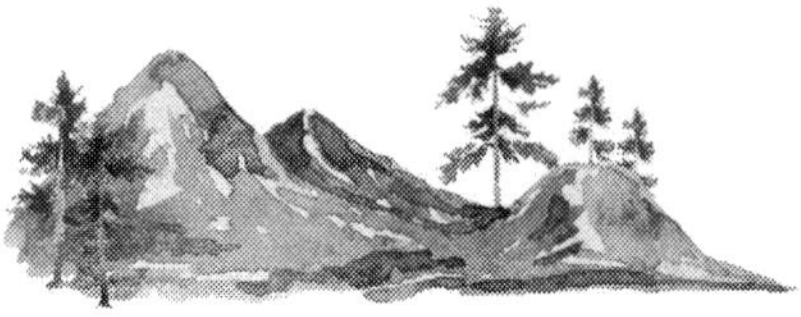

Date: ______	From: ______	Beginning Mileage: ______
Weather:	To: ______	Ending Mileage: ______
	Route Taken: ______	Total Miles Traveled:

Campground Information

Name: ______	Our Rating: ☆ ☆ ☆ ☆ ☆
Address: ______	GPS: ______
Phone: ______	Altitude: ______
Site # ______ $ ______ ☐ Day ☐ Week ☐ Month	Cell Service / Carrier: ______

☐ First Visit	☐ Return Visit	☐ Easy Access	
☐ Site Level	☐ Back-in	☐ Pull-through	
☐ 15 amp	☐ 30 amp	☐ 50 amp	
☐ Water	☐ Sewer	☐ Shade	☐ Sun
☐ Paved	☐ Sand / Grass	☐ Gravel	
☐ Picnic Table	☐ Fire ring	☐ Trees	☐ Lawn
☐ Patio	☐ Kid Friendly	☐ Pet Friendly	
☐ Store	☐ Cafe	☐ Firewood	
☐ Ice	☐ Security	☐ Quiet	☐ Noisy

☐ Antenna Reception ☐ Satellite TV ☐ Cable TV

☐ WIFI Available ☐ Free ☐ Fee $ ______

Memberships: ______

Amenities: ______

Location	☺ 😐 ☹	Water Pressure	☺ 😐 ☹
Restrooms	☺ 😐 ☹	Laundry	☺ 😐 ☹
Pool	☺ 😐 ☹	Hot Tub	☺ 😐 ☹

Places Visited / Activities:

People Met / New Friends:

Food, Dining & Restaurants:

Highlights / Memorable Events:

Places To Go & Things To Do for Next Time:

NOTES:

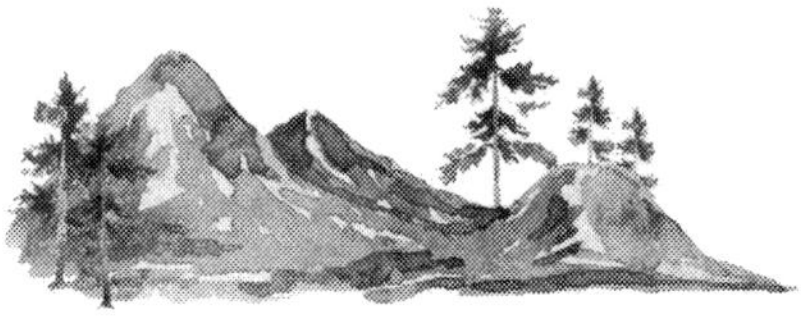

Date:	From:	Beginning Mileage:
Weather:	To:	Ending Mileage:
	Route Taken:	Total Miles Traveled:

Campground Information

Name:		Our Rating: ☆ ☆ ☆ ☆ ☆	
Address:		GPS:	
Phone:		Altitude:	
Site #	$ ☐ Day ☐ Week ☐ Month	Cell Service / Carrier:	

☐ First Visit	☐ Return Visit	☐ Easy Access	
☐ Site Level	☐ Back-in	☐ Pull-through	
☐ 15 amp	☐ 30 amp	☐ 50 amp	
☐ Water	☐ Sewer	☐ Shade	☐ Sun
☐ Paved	☐ Sand / Grass	☐ Gravel	
☐ Picnic Table	☐ Fire ring	☐ Trees	☐ Lawn
☐ Patio	☐ Kid Friendly	☐ Pet Friendly	
☐ Store	☐ Cafe	☐ Firewood	
☐ Ice	☐ Security	☐ Quiet	☐ Noisy

☐ Antenna Reception ☐ Satellite TV ☐ Cable TV

☐ WIFI Available ☐ Free ☐ Fee $

Memberships:

Amenities:

Location	☺ 😐 ☹	Water Pressure	☺ 😐 ☹
Restrooms	☺ 😐 ☹	Laundry	☺ 😐 ☹
Pool	☺ 😐 ☹	Hot Tub	☺ 😐 ☹

Places Visited / Activities:

People Met / New Friends:

Food, Dining & Restaurants:

Highlights / Memorable Events:

Places To Go & Things To Do for Next Time:

Notes:

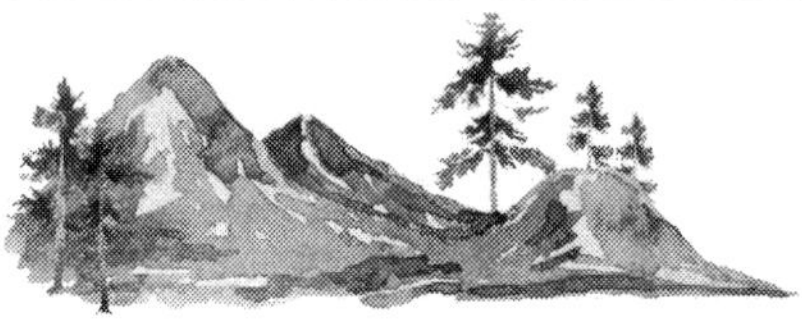

Date: ____	From: ____	Beginning Mileage: ____
Weather:	To: ____	Ending Mileage: ____
	Route Taken: ____	Total Miles Traveled:

Campground Information

Name: ____		Our Rating: ☆ ☆ ☆ ☆ ☆	
Address: ____		GPS: ____	
Phone: ____		Altitude: ____	
Site # ____	$ ____	☐ Day ☐ Week ☐ Month	Cell Service / Carrier: ____
☐ First Visit	☐ Return Visit	☐ Easy Access	☐ Antenna Reception ☐ Satellite TV ☐ Cable TV
☐ Site Level	☐ Back-in	☐ Pull-through	☐ WIFI Available ☐ Free ☐ Fee $ ____
☐ 15 amp	☐ 30 amp	☐ 50 amp	
☐ Water	☐ Sewer	☐ Shade ☐ Sun	Memberships: ____
☐ Paved	☐ Sand / Grass	☐ Gravel	Amenities: ____
☐ Picnic Table	☐ Fire ring	☐ Trees ☐ Lawn	
☐ Patio	☐ Kid Friendly	☐ Pet Friendly	Location ☺ 😐 ☹ Water Pressure ☺ 😐 ☹
☐ Store	☐ Cafe	☐ Firewood	Restrooms ☺ 😐 ☹ Laundry ☺ 😐 ☹
☐ Ice	☐ Security	☐ Quiet ☐ Noisy	Pool ☺ 😐 ☹ Hot Tub ☺ 😐 ☹

Places Visited / Activities:

People Met / New Friends:

Food, Dining & Restaurants:

Highlights / Memorable Events:

Places To Go & Things To Do for Next Time:

NOTES:

Date: ______

Weather:

From: ______

To: ______

Route Taken: ______

Beginning Mileage: ______

Ending Mileage: ______

Total Miles Traveled:

Campground Information

Name: ______

Address: ______

Phone: ______

Site # ______ $ ______ ☐ Day ☐ Week ☐ Month

☐ First Visit ☐ Return Visit ☐ Easy Access
☐ Site Level ☐ Back-in ☐ Pull-through
☐ 15 amp ☐ 30 amp ☐ 50 amp
☐ Water ☐ Sewer ☐ Shade ☐ Sun
☐ Paved ☐ Sand / Grass ☐ Gravel
☐ Picnic Table ☐ Fire ring ☐ Trees ☐ Lawn
☐ Patio ☐ Kid Friendly ☐ Pet Friendly
☐ Store ☐ Cafe ☐ Firewood
☐ Ice ☐ Security ☐ Quiet ☐ Noisy

Our Rating: ☆ ☆ ☆ ☆ ☆

GPS: ______

Altitude: ______

Cell Service / Carrier: ______

☐ Antenna Reception ☐ Satellite TV ☐ Cable TV
☐ WIFI Available ☐ Free ☐ Fee $ ______

Memberships: ______

Amenities: ______

Location ☺ 😐 ☹ Water Pressure ☺ 😐 ☹
Restrooms ☺ 😐 ☹ Laundry ☺ 😐 ☹
Pool ☺ 😐 ☹ Hot Tub ☺ 😐 ☹

Places Visited / Activities:

People Met / New Friends:

Food, Dining & Restaurants:

Highlights / Memorable Events:

Places To Go & Things To Do for Next Time:

Notes:

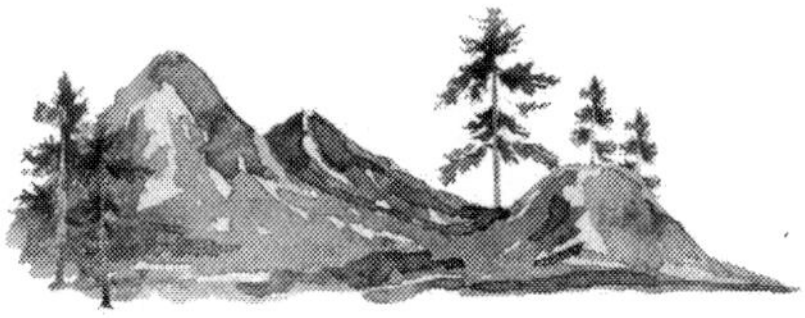

Date: ______

Weather:

From: ______

To: ______

Route Taken: ______

Beginning Mileage: ______

Ending Mileage: ______

Total Miles Traveled:

Campground Information

Name: ______

Address: ______

Phone: ______

Site # ______ $ ______ ☐ Day ☐ Week ☐ Month

☐ First Visit ☐ Return Visit ☐ Easy Access

☐ Site Level ☐ Back-in ☐ Pull-through

☐ 15 amp ☐ 30 amp ☐ 50 amp

☐ Water ☐ Sewer ☐ Shade ☐ Sun

☐ Paved ☐ Sand / Grass ☐ Gravel

☐ Picnic Table ☐ Fire ring ☐ Trees ☐ Lawn

☐ Patio ☐ Kid Friendly ☐ Pet Friendly

☐ Store ☐ Cafe ☐ Firewood

☐ Ice ☐ Security ☐ Quiet ☐ Noisy

Our Rating: ☆ ☆ ☆ ☆ ☆

GPS: ______

Altitude: ______

Cell Service / Carrier: ______

☐ Antenna Reception ☐ Satellite TV ☐ Cable TV

☐ WIFI Available ☐ Free ☐ Fee $ ______

Memberships: ______

Amenities: ______

Location ☺ 😐 ☹ Water Pressure ☺ 😐 ☹

Restrooms ☺ 😐 ☹ Laundry ☺ 😐 ☹

Pool ☺ 😐 ☹ Hot Tub ☺ 😐 ☹

Places Visited / Activities:

People Met / New Friends:

Food, Dining & Restaurants:

Highlights / Memorable Events:

Places To Go & Things To Do for Next Time:

Notes:

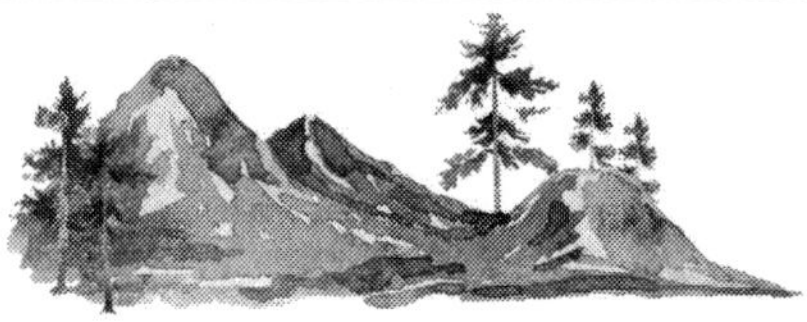

Date:	From:	Beginning Mileage:
Weather:	To:	Ending Mileage:
	Route Taken:	Total Miles Traveled:

Campground Information

Name:		Our Rating: ☆ ☆ ☆ ☆ ☆	
Address:		GPS:	
Phone:		Altitude:	
Site #	$	☐ Day ☐ Week ☐ Month	Cell Service / Carrier:

☐ First Visit	☐ Return Visit	☐ Easy Access	
☐ Site Level	☐ Back-in	☐ Pull-through	
☐ 15 amp	☐ 30 amp	☐ 50 amp	
☐ Water	☐ Sewer	☐ Shade	☐ Sun
☐ Paved	☐ Sand / Grass	☐ Gravel	
☐ Picnic Table	☐ Fire ring	☐ Trees	☐ Lawn
☐ Patio	☐ Kid Friendly	☐ Pet Friendly	
☐ Store	☐ Cafe	☐ Firewood	
☐ Ice	☐ Security	☐ Quiet	☐ Noisy

☐ Antenna Reception ☐ Satellite TV ☐ Cable TV

☐ WIFI Available ☐ Free ☐ Fee $

Memberships:

Amenities:

Location	☺	😐	☹	Water Pressure	☺	😐	☹
Restrooms	☺	😐	☹	Laundry	☺	😐	☹
Pool	☺	😐	☹	Hot Tub	☺	😐	☹

Places Visited / Activities:

People Met / New Friends:

Food, Dining & Restaurants:

Highlights / Memorable Events:

Places To Go & Things To Do for Next Time:

Notes:

Date:

Weather:

From:

To:

Route Taken:

Beginning Mileage:

Ending Mileage:

Total Miles Traveled:

Campground Information

Name:

Address:

Phone:

Site # $ ☐ Day ☐ Week ☐ Month

☐ First Visit	☐ Return Visit	☐ Easy Access	
☐ Site Level	☐ Back-in	☐ Pull-through	
☐ 15 amp	☐ 30 amp	☐ 50 amp	
☐ Water	☐ Sewer	☐ Shade	☐ Sun
☐ Paved	☐ Sand / Grass	☐ Gravel	
☐ Picnic Table	☐ Fire ring	☐ Trees	☐ Lawn
☐ Patio	☐ Kid Friendly	☐ Pet Friendly	
☐ Store	☐ Cafe	☐ Firewood	
☐ Ice	☐ Security	☐ Quiet	☐ Noisy

Our Rating: ☆ ☆ ☆ ☆ ☆

GPS:

Altitude:

Cell Service / Carrier:

☐ Antenna Reception ☐ Satellite TV ☐ Cable TV

☐ WIFI Available ☐ Free ☐ Fee $

Memberships:

Amenities:

Location	☺	😐	☹	Water Pressure	☺	😐	☹
Restrooms	☺	😐	☹	Laundry	☺	😐	☹
Pool	☺	😐	☹	Hot Tub	☺	😐	☹

Places Visited / Activities:

People Met / New Friends:

Food, Dining & Restaurants:

Highlights / Memorable Events:

Places To Go & Things To Do for Next Time:

Notes:

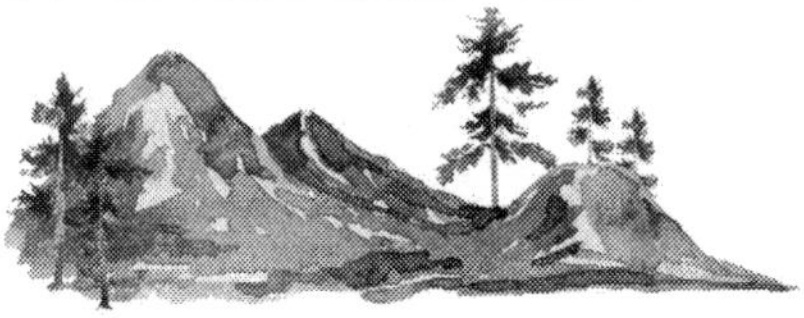

Date: ______ Weather:	From: ______ To: ______ Route Taken: ______	Beginning Mileage: ______ Ending Mileage: ______ Total Miles Traveled:

Campground Information

Name: ______	Our Rating: ☆ ☆ ☆ ☆ ☆
Address: ______	GPS: ______
Phone: ______	Altitude: ______
Site # ______ $ ______ ☐ Day ☐ Week ☐ Month	Cell Service / Carrier: ______
☐ First Visit ☐ Return Visit ☐ Easy Access	☐ Antenna Reception ☐ Satellite TV ☐ Cable TV
☐ Site Level ☐ Back-in ☐ Pull-through	☐ WIFI Available ☐ Free ☐ Fee $ ______
☐ 15 amp ☐ 30 amp ☐ 50 amp	
☐ Water ☐ Sewer ☐ Shade ☐ Sun	Memberships: ______
☐ Paved ☐ Sand / Grass ☐ Gravel	Amenities: ______
☐ Picnic Table ☐ Fire ring ☐ Trees ☐ Lawn	
☐ Patio ☐ Kid Friendly ☐ Pet Friendly	Location ☺ 😐 ☹ Water Pressure ☺ 😐 ☹
☐ Store ☐ Cafe ☐ Firewood	Restrooms ☺ 😐 ☹ Laundry ☺ 😐 ☹
☐ Ice ☐ Security ☐ Quiet ☐ Noisy	Pool ☺ 😐 ☹ Hot Tub ☺ 😐 ☹

Places Visited / Activities:

People Met / New Friends:

Food, Dining & Restaurants:

Highlights / Memorable Events:

Places To Go & Things To Do for Next Time:

Notes:

Date: ______ Weather:	From: ______ To: ______ Route Taken: ______	Beginning Mileage: ______ Ending Mileage: ______ Total Miles Traveled:

Campground Information

Name:	Our Rating: ☆ ☆ ☆ ☆ ☆
Address:	GPS:
Phone:	Altitude:
Site # ______ $ ______ ☐ Day ☐ Week ☐ Month	Cell Service / Carrier:
☐ First Visit ☐ Return Visit ☐ Easy Access	☐ Antenna Reception ☐ Satellite TV ☐ Cable TV
☐ Site Level ☐ Back-in ☐ Pull-through	☐ WIFI Available ☐ Free ☐ Fee $ ______
☐ 15 amp ☐ 30 amp ☐ 50 amp	Memberships:
☐ Water ☐ Sewer ☐ Shade ☐ Sun	Amenities:
☐ Paved ☐ Sand / Grass ☐ Gravel	
☐ Picnic Table ☐ Fire ring ☐ Trees ☐ Lawn	Location ☺ 😐 ☹ Water Pressure ☺ 😐 ☹
☐ Patio ☐ Kid Friendly ☐ Pet Friendly	Restrooms ☺ 😐 ☹ Laundry ☺ 😐 ☹
☐ Store ☐ Cafe ☐ Firewood	
☐ Ice ☐ Security ☐ Quiet ☐ Noisy	Pool ☺ 😐 ☹ Hot Tub ☺ 😐 ☹

Places Visited / Activities: ______

People Met / New Friends: ______

Food, Dining & Restaurants: ______

Highlights / Memorable Events: ______

Places To Go & Things To Do for Next Time: ______

Notes:

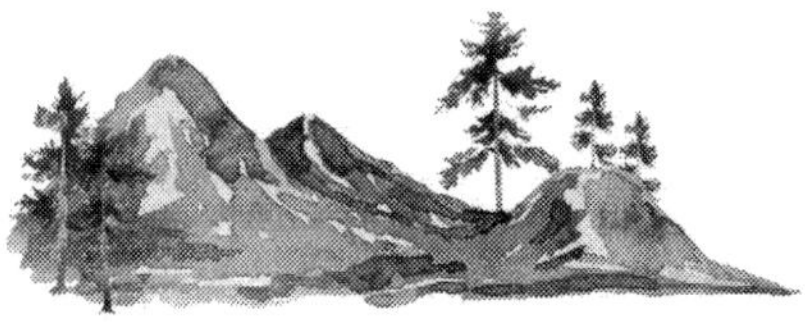

Date:	From:	Beginning Mileage:
Weather:	To:	Ending Mileage:
	Route Taken:	Total Miles Traveled:

Campground Information

Name:	Our Rating: ☆ ☆ ☆ ☆ ☆
Address:	GPS:
Phone:	Altitude:
Site # ___ $ ___ ☐ Day ☐ Week ☐ Month	Cell Service / Carrier:

☐ First Visit	☐ Return Visit	☐ Easy Access	
☐ Site Level	☐ Back-in	☐ Pull-through	
☐ 15 amp	☐ 30 amp	☐ 50 amp	
☐ Water	☐ Sewer	☐ Shade	☐ Sun
☐ Paved	☐ Sand / Grass	☐ Gravel	
☐ Picnic Table	☐ Fire ring	☐ Trees	☐ Lawn
☐ Patio	☐ Kid Friendly	☐ Pet Friendly	
☐ Store	☐ Cafe	☐ Firewood	
☐ Ice	☐ Security	☐ Quiet	☐ Noisy

☐ Antenna Reception ☐ Satellite TV ☐ Cable TV

☐ WIFI Available ☐ Free ☐ Fee $

Memberships:

Amenities:

Location	☺ 😐 ☹	Water Pressure	☺ 😐 ☹
Restrooms	☺ 😐 ☹	Laundry	☺ 😐 ☹
Pool	☺ 😐 ☹	Hot Tub	☺ 😐 ☹

Places Visited / Activities:

People Met / New Friends:

Food, Dining & Restaurants:

Highlights / Memorable Events:

Places To Go & Things To Do for Next Time:

Notes:

Date: ____________

Weather:

From: ____________

To: ____________

Route Taken: ____________

Beginning Mileage:

Ending Mileage:

Total Miles Traveled:

Campground Information

Name: ____________

Address: ____________

Phone: ____________

Site # ________ $ ________ ☐ Day ☐ Week ☐ Month

☐ First Visit	☐ Return Visit	☐ Easy Access	
☐ Site Level	☐ Back-in	☐ Pull-through	
☐ 15 amp	☐ 30 amp	☐ 50 amp	
☐ Water	☐ Sewer	☐ Shade	☐ Sun
☐ Paved	☐ Sand / Grass	☐ Gravel	
☐ Picnic Table	☐ Fire ring	☐ Trees	☐ Lawn
☐ Patio	☐ Kid Friendly	☐ Pet Friendly	
☐ Store	☐ Cafe	☐ Firewood	
☐ Ice	☐ Security	☐ Quiet	☐ Noisy

Our Rating: ☆ ☆ ☆ ☆ ☆

GPS: ____________

Altitude: ____________

Cell Service / Carrier: ____________

☐ Antenna Reception ☐ Satellite TV ☐ Cable TV

☐ WIFI Available ☐ Free ☐ Fee $ ________

Memberships: ____________

Amenities: ____________

Location	☺	😐	☹	Water Pressure	☺	😐	☹
Restrooms	☺	😐	☹	Laundry	☺	😐	☹
Pool	☺	😐	☹	Hot Tub	☺	😐	☹

Places Visited / Activities:

People Met / New Friends:

Food, Dining & Restaurants:

Highlights / Memorable Events:

Places To Go & Things To Do for Next Time:

Notes:

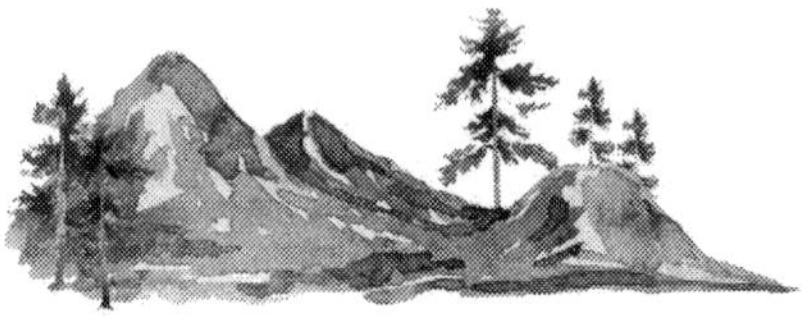

Date: ____________

Weather:

From: ____________

To: ____________

Route Taken: ____________

____

Beginning Mileage: ____________

Ending Mileage: ____________

Total Miles Traveled:

Campground Information

Name: ____________

Address: ____________

Phone: ____________

Site # ________ $ ________ ☐ Day ☐ Week ☐ Month

☐ First Visit ☐ Return Visit ☐ Easy Access

☐ Site Level ☐ Back-in ☐ Pull-through

☐ 15 amp ☐ 30 amp ☐ 50 amp

☐ Water ☐ Sewer ☐ Shade ☐ Sun

☐ Paved ☐ Sand / Grass ☐ Gravel

☐ Picnic Table ☐ Fire ring ☐ Trees ☐ Lawn

☐ Patio ☐ Kid Friendly ☐ Pet Friendly

☐ Store ☐ Cafe ☐ Firewood

☐ Ice ☐ Security ☐ Quiet ☐ Noisy

Our Rating: ☆ ☆ ☆ ☆ ☆

GPS: ____________

Altitude: ____________

Cell Service / Carrier: ____________

☐ Antenna Reception ☐ Satellite TV ☐ Cable TV

☐ WIFI Available ☐ Free ☐ Fee $ ________

Memberships: ____________

Amenities: ____________

Location ☺ 😐 ☹ Water Pressure ☺ 😐 ☹

Restrooms ☺ 😐 ☹ Laundry ☺ 😐 ☹

Pool ☺ 😐 ☹ Hot Tub ☺ 😐 ☹

Places Visited / Activities:

People Met / New Friends:

Food, Dining & Restaurants:

Highlights / Memorable Events:

Places To Go & Things To Do for Next Time:

Notes:

Date:

Weather:

From:

To:

Route Taken:

Beginning Mileage:

Ending Mileage:

Total Miles Traveled:

Campground Information

Name:

Address:

Phone:

Site # $ ☐ Day ☐ Week ☐ Month

☐ First Visit ☐ Return Visit ☐ Easy Access
☐ Site Level ☐ Back-in ☐ Pull-through
☐ 15 amp ☐ 30 amp ☐ 50 amp
☐ Water ☐ Sewer ☐ Shade ☐ Sun
☐ Paved ☐ Sand / Grass ☐ Gravel
☐ Picnic Table ☐ Fire ring ☐ Trees ☐ Lawn
☐ Patio ☐ Kid Friendly ☐ Pet Friendly
☐ Store ☐ Cafe ☐ Firewood
☐ Ice ☐ Security ☐ Quiet ☐ Noisy

Our Rating: ☆ ☆ ☆ ☆ ☆

GPS:

Altitude:

Cell Service / Carrier:

☐ Antenna Reception ☐ Satellite TV ☐ Cable TV
☐ WIFI Available ☐ Free ☐ Fee $

Memberships:

Amenities:

Location ☺ 😐 ☹ Water Pressure ☺ 😐 ☹
Restrooms ☺ 😐 ☹ Laundry ☺ 😐 ☹
Pool ☺ 😐 ☹ Hot Tub ☺ 😐 ☹

Places Visited / Activities:

People Met / New Friends:

Food, Dining & Restaurants:

Highlights / Memorable Events:

Places To Go & Things To Do for Next Time:

Notes:

Date:	From:	Beginning Mileage:
Weather:	To:	Ending Mileage:
	Route Taken:	Total Miles Traveled:

Campground Information

Name:	Our Rating: ☆ ☆ ☆ ☆ ☆
Address:	GPS:
Phone:	Altitude:
Site # ____ $ ____ ☐ Day ☐ Week ☐ Month	Cell Service / Carrier:

☐ First Visit	☐ Return Visit	☐ Easy Access	
☐ Site Level	☐ Back-in	☐ Pull-through	
☐ 15 amp	☐ 30 amp	☐ 50 amp	
☐ Water	☐ Sewer	☐ Shade	☐ Sun
☐ Paved	☐ Sand / Grass	☐ Gravel	
☐ Picnic Table	☐ Fire ring	☐ Trees	☐ Lawn
☐ Patio	☐ Kid Friendly	☐ Pet Friendly	
☐ Store	☐ Cafe	☐ Firewood	
☐ Ice	☐ Security	☐ Quiet	☐ Noisy

☐ Antenna Reception ☐ Satellite TV ☐ Cable TV

☐ WIFI Available ☐ Free ☐ Fee $

Memberships:

Amenities:

Location	☺	😐	☹	Water Pressure	☺	😐	☹
Restrooms	☺	😐	☹	Laundry	☺	😐	☹
Pool	☺	😐	☹	Hot Tub	☺	😐	☹

Places Visited / Activities:

People Met / New Friends:

Food, Dining & Restaurants:

Highlights / Memorable Events:

Places To Go & Things To Do for Next Time:

Notes:

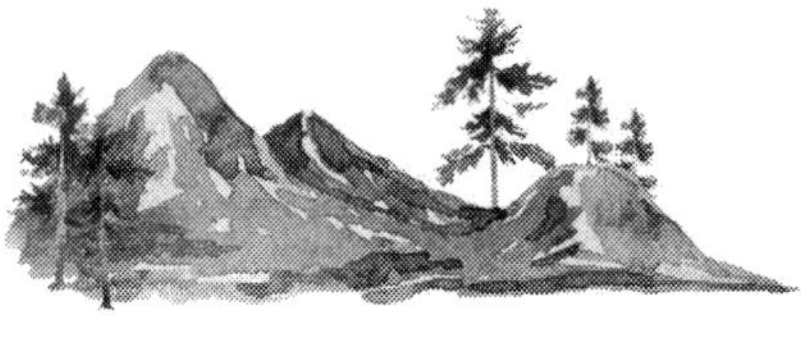

Date: ______

Weather:

From: ______
To: ______
Route Taken: ______

Beginning Mileage: ______
Ending Mileage: ______
Total Miles Traveled:

Campground Information

Name: ______
Address: ______
Phone: ______
Site # ______ $ ______ ☐ Day ☐ Week ☐ Month

☐ First Visit	☐ Return Visit	☐ Easy Access	
☐ Site Level	☐ Back-in	☐ Pull-through	
☐ 15 amp	☐ 30 amp	☐ 50 amp	
☐ Water	☐ Sewer	☐ Shade	☐ Sun
☐ Paved	☐ Sand / Grass	☐ Gravel	
☐ Picnic Table	☐ Fire ring	☐ Trees	☐ Lawn
☐ Patio	☐ Kid Friendly	☐ Pet Friendly	
☐ Store	☐ Cafe	☐ Firewood	
☐ Ice	☐ Security	☐ Quiet	☐ Noisy

Our Rating: ☆ ☆ ☆ ☆ ☆
GPS: ______
Altitude: ______
Cell Service / Carrier: ______

☐ Antenna Reception ☐ Satellite TV ☐ Cable TV
☐ WIFI Available ☐ Free ☐ Fee $ ______

Memberships: ______
Amenities: ______

Location	☺	😐	☹	Water Pressure	☺	😐	☹
Restrooms	☺	😐	☹	Laundry	☺	😐	☹
Pool	☺	😐	☹	Hot Tub	☺	😐	☹

Places Visited / Activities:

People Met / New Friends:

Food, Dining & Restaurants:

Highlights / Memorable Events:

Places To Go & Things To Do for Next Time:

NOTES:

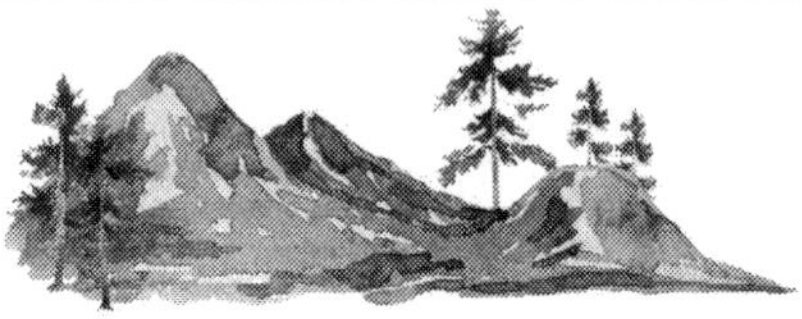

Date: ______ From: ______ Beginning Mileage: ______

Weather: To: ______ Ending Mileage: ______

Route Taken: ______ Total Miles Traveled: ______

Campground Information

Name:		Our Rating: ☆ ☆ ☆ ☆ ☆	
Address:		GPS:	
Phone:		Altitude:	
Site # ____ $ ____ ☐ Day ☐ Week ☐ Month		Cell Service / Carrier:	

☐ First Visit	☐ Return Visit	☐ Easy Access	
☐ Site Level	☐ Back-in	☐ Pull-through	
☐ 15 amp	☐ 30 amp	☐ 50 amp	
☐ Water	☐ Sewer	☐ Shade	☐ Sun
☐ Paved	☐ Sand / Grass	☐ Gravel	
☐ Picnic Table	☐ Fire ring	☐ Trees	☐ Lawn
☐ Patio	☐ Kid Friendly	☐ Pet Friendly	
☐ Store	☐ Cafe	☐ Firewood	
☐ Ice	☐ Security	☐ Quiet	☐ Noisy

☐ Antenna Reception ☐ Satellite TV ☐ Cable TV

☐ WIFI Available ☐ Free ☐ Fee $ ______

Memberships: ______

Amenities: ______

Location	☺ 😐 ☹	Water Pressure	☺ 😐 ☹
Restrooms	☺ 😐 ☹	Laundry	☺ 😐 ☹
Pool	☺ 😐 ☹	Hot Tub	☺ 😐 ☹

Places Visited / Activities:

People Met / New Friends:

Food, Dining & Restaurants:

Highlights / Memorable Events:

Places To Go & Things To Do for Next Time:

NOTES:

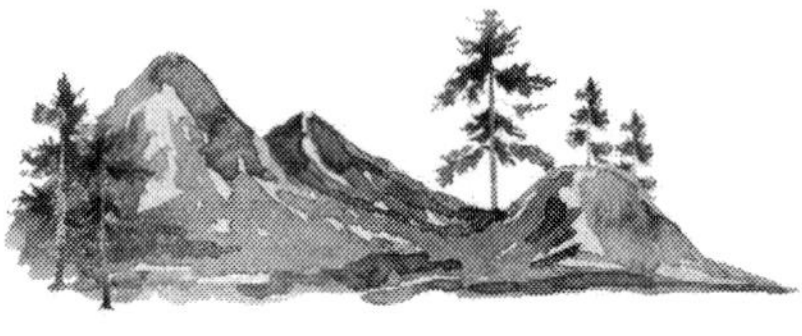

Date: ____________

Weather:

From: ____________

To: ____________

Route Taken: ____________

Beginning Mileage: ____________

Ending Mileage: ____________

Total Miles Traveled:

Campground Information

Name: ____________

Address: ____________

Phone: ____________

Site # ________ $ ________ ☐ Day ☐ Week ☐ Month

☐ First Visit ☐ Return Visit ☐ Easy Access
☐ Site Level ☐ Back-in ☐ Pull-through
☐ 15 amp ☐ 30 amp ☐ 50 amp
☐ Water ☐ Sewer ☐ Shade ☐ Sun
☐ Paved ☐ Sand / Grass ☐ Gravel
☐ Picnic Table ☐ Fire ring ☐ Trees ☐ Lawn
☐ Patio ☐ Kid Friendly ☐ Pet Friendly
☐ Store ☐ Cafe ☐ Firewood
☐ Ice ☐ Security ☐ Quiet ☐ Noisy

Our Rating: ☆ ☆ ☆ ☆ ☆

GPS: ____________

Altitude: ____________

Cell Service / Carrier: ____________

☐ Antenna Reception ☐ Satellite TV ☐ Cable TV
☐ WIFI Available ☐ Free ☐ Fee $ ________

Memberships: ____________

Amenities: ____________

Location ☺ 😐 ☹ Water Pressure ☺ 😐 ☹
Restrooms ☺ 😐 ☹ Laundry ☺ 😐 ☹
Pool ☺ 😐 ☹ Hot Tub ☺ 😐 ☹

Places Visited / Activities:

People Met / New Friends:

Food, Dining & Restaurants:

Highlights / Memorable Events:

Places To Go & Things To Do for Next Time:

Notes:

Date:

Weather:

From:

To:

Route Taken:

Beginning Mileage:

Ending Mileage:

Total Miles Traveled:

Campground Information

Name:

Address:

Phone:

Site # $ ☐ Day ☐ Week ☐ Month

☐ First Visit ☐ Return Visit ☐ Easy Access
☐ Site Level ☐ Back-in ☐ Pull-through
☐ 15 amp ☐ 30 amp ☐ 50 amp
☐ Water ☐ Sewer ☐ Shade ☐ Sun
☐ Paved ☐ Sand / Grass ☐ Gravel
☐ Picnic Table ☐ Fire ring ☐ Trees ☐ Lawn
☐ Patio ☐ Kid Friendly ☐ Pet Friendly
☐ Store ☐ Cafe ☐ Firewood
☐ Ice ☐ Security ☐ Quiet ☐ Noisy

Our Rating: ☆ ☆ ☆ ☆ ☆

GPS:

Altitude:

Cell Service / Carrier:

☐ Antenna Reception ☐ Satellite TV ☐ Cable TV
☐ WIFI Available ☐ Free ☐ Fee $

Memberships:

Amenities:

Location ☺ 😐 ☹ Water Pressure ☺ 😐 ☹
Restrooms ☺ 😐 ☹ Laundry ☺ 😐 ☹
Pool ☺ 😐 ☹ Hot Tub ☺ 😐 ☹

Places Visited / Activities:

People Met / New Friends:

Food, Dining & Restaurants:

Highlights / Memorable Events:

Places To Go & Things To Do for Next Time:

Notes:

Date:	From:	Beginning Mileage:
Weather:	To:	Ending Mileage:
	Route Taken:	Total Miles Traveled:

Campground Information

Name:	Our Rating: ☆ ☆ ☆ ☆ ☆
Address:	GPS:
Phone:	Altitude:
Site # ___ $ ___ ☐ Day ☐ Week ☐ Month	Cell Service / Carrier:
☐ First Visit ☐ Return Visit ☐ Easy Access	☐ Antenna Reception ☐ Satellite TV ☐ Cable TV
☐ Site Level ☐ Back-in ☐ Pull-through	☐ WIFI Available ☐ Free ☐ Fee $
☐ 15 amp ☐ 30 amp ☐ 50 amp	Memberships:
☐ Water ☐ Sewer ☐ Shade ☐ Sun	Amenities:
☐ Paved ☐ Sand / Grass ☐ Gravel	Location ☺ 😐 ☹ Water Pressure ☺ 😐 ☹
☐ Picnic Table ☐ Fire ring ☐ Trees ☐ Lawn	Restrooms ☺ 😐 ☹ Laundry ☺ 😐 ☹
☐ Patio ☐ Kid Friendly ☐ Pet Friendly	Pool ☺ 😐 ☹ Hot Tub ☺ 😐 ☹
☐ Store ☐ Cafe ☐ Firewood	
☐ Ice ☐ Security ☐ Quiet ☐ Noisy	

Places Visited / Activities:

People Met / New Friends:

Food, Dining & Restaurants:

Highlights / Memorable Events:

Places To Go & Things To Do for Next Time:

Notes:

Date:

Weather:

From:

To:

Route Taken:

Beginning Mileage:

Ending Mileage:

Total Miles Traveled:

Campground Information

Name:

Address:

Phone:

Site # $ ☐ Day ☐ Week ☐ Month

☐ First Visit ☐ Return Visit ☐ Easy Access
☐ Site Level ☐ Back-in ☐ Pull-through
☐ 15 amp ☐ 30 amp ☐ 50 amp
☐ Water ☐ Sewer ☐ Shade ☐ Sun
☐ Paved ☐ Sand / Grass ☐ Gravel
☐ Picnic Table ☐ Fire ring ☐ Trees ☐ Lawn
☐ Patio ☐ Kid Friendly ☐ Pet Friendly
☐ Store ☐ Cafe ☐ Firewood
☐ Ice ☐ Security ☐ Quiet ☐ Noisy

Our Rating: ☆ ☆ ☆ ☆ ☆

GPS:

Altitude:

Cell Service / Carrier:

☐ Antenna Reception ☐ Satellite TV ☐ Cable TV
☐ WIFI Available ☐ Free ☐ Fee $

Memberships:

Amenities:

Location ☺ 😐 ☹ Water Pressure ☺ 😐 ☹
Restrooms ☺ 😐 ☹ Laundry ☺ 😐 ☹
Pool ☺ 😐 ☹ Hot Tub ☺ 😐 ☹

Places Visited / Activities:

People Met / New Friends:

Food, Dining & Restaurants:

Highlights / Memorable Events:

Places To Go & Things To Do for Next Time:

NOTES:

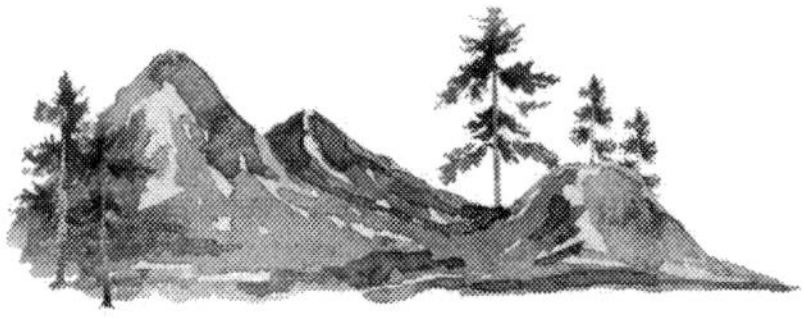

Date:

Weather:

From:

To:

Route Taken:

Beginning Mileage:

Ending Mileage:

Total Miles Traveled:

Campground Information

Name:

Address:

Phone:

Site # $ ☐ Day ☐ Week ☐ Month

☐ First Visit ☐ Return Visit ☐ Easy Access

☐ Site Level ☐ Back-in ☐ Pull-through

☐ 15 amp ☐ 30 amp ☐ 50 amp

☐ Water ☐ Sewer ☐ Shade ☐ Sun

☐ Paved ☐ Sand / Grass ☐ Gravel

☐ Picnic Table ☐ Fire ring ☐ Trees ☐ Lawn

☐ Patio ☐ Kid Friendly ☐ Pet Friendly

☐ Store ☐ Cafe ☐ Firewood

☐ Ice ☐ Security ☐ Quiet ☐ Noisy

Our Rating: ☆ ☆ ☆ ☆ ☆

GPS:

Altitude:

Cell Service / Carrier:

☐ Antenna Reception ☐ Satellite TV ☐ Cable TV

☐ WIFI Available ☐ Free ☐ Fee $

Memberships:

Amenities:

Location ☺ 😐 ☹ Water Pressure ☺ 😐 ☹

Restrooms ☺ 😐 ☹ Laundry ☺ 😐 ☹

Pool ☺ 😐 ☹ Hot Tub ☺ 😐 ☹

Places Visited / Activities:

People Met / New Friends:

Food, Dining & Restaurants:

Highlights / Memorable Events:

Places To Go & Things To Do for Next Time:

Notes:

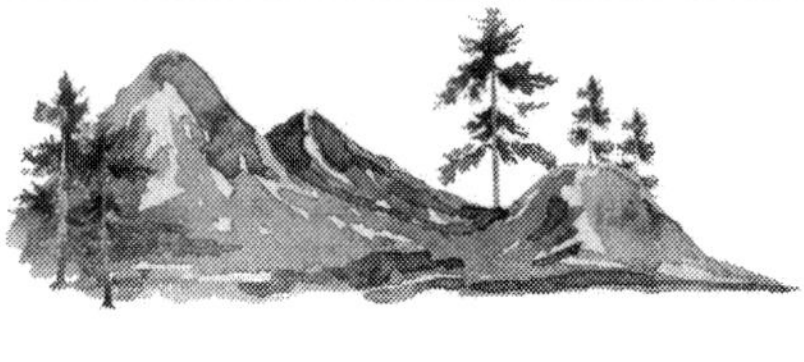

Date:	From:	Beginning Mileage:
Weather:	To:	Ending Mileage:
	Route Taken:	Total Miles Traveled:

Campground Information

Name:			
Address:			
Phone:			
Site #	$	☐ Day ☐ Week	☐ Month
☐ First Visit	☐ Return Visit	☐ Easy Access	
☐ Site Level	☐ Back-in	☐ Pull-through	
☐ 15 amp	☐ 30 amp	☐ 50 amp	
☐ Water	☐ Sewer	☐ Shade	☐ Sun
☐ Paved	☐ Sand / Grass	☐ Gravel	
☐ Picnic Table	☐ Fire ring	☐ Trees	☐ Lawn
☐ Patio	☐ Kid Friendly	☐ Pet Friendly	
☐ Store	☐ Cafe	☐ Firewood	
☐ Ice	☐ Security	☐ Quiet	☐ Noisy

Our Rating: ☆ ☆ ☆ ☆ ☆

GPS:

Altitude:

Cell Service / Carrier:

☐ Antenna Reception ☐ Satellite TV ☐ Cable TV

☐ WIFI Available ☐ Free ☐ Fee $

Memberships:

Amenities:

Location	☺ 😐 ☹	Water Pressure	☺ 😐 ☹
Restrooms	☺ 😐 ☹	Laundry	☺ 😐 ☹
Pool	☺ 😐 ☹	Hot Tub	☺ 😐 ☹

Places Visited / Activities:

People Met / New Friends:

Food, Dining & Restaurants:

Highlights / Memorable Events:

Places To Go & Things To Do for Next Time:

NOTES:

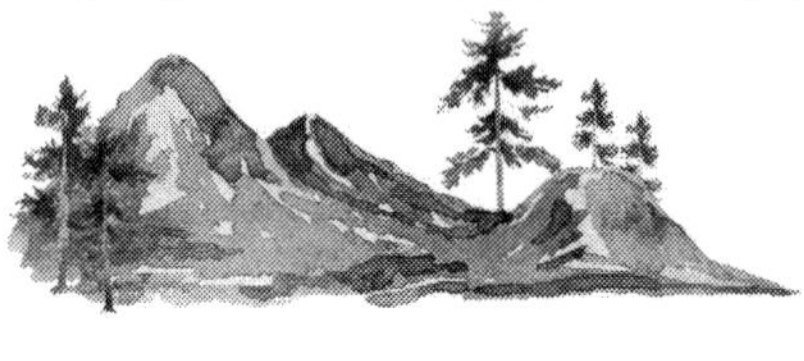

Date:

Weather:

From:

To:

Route Taken:

Beginning Mileage:

Ending Mileage:

Total Miles Traveled:

Campground Information

Name:

Address:

Phone:

Site # $ ☐ Day ☐ Week ☐ Month

☐ First Visit ☐ Return Visit ☐ Easy Access

☐ Site Level ☐ Back-in ☐ Pull-through

☐ 15 amp ☐ 30 amp ☐ 50 amp

☐ Water ☐ Sewer ☐ Shade ☐ Sun

☐ Paved ☐ Sand / Grass ☐ Gravel

☐ Picnic Table ☐ Fire ring ☐ Trees ☐ Lawn

☐ Patio ☐ Kid Friendly ☐ Pet Friendly

☐ Store ☐ Cafe ☐ Firewood

☐ Ice ☐ Security ☐ Quiet ☐ Noisy

Our Rating: ☆ ☆ ☆ ☆ ☆

GPS:

Altitude:

Cell Service / Carrier:

☐ Antenna Reception ☐ Satellite TV ☐ Cable TV

☐ WIFI Available ☐ Free ☐ Fee $

Memberships:

Amenities:

Location ☺ 😐 ☹ Water Pressure ☺ 😐 ☹

Restrooms ☺ 😐 ☹ Laundry ☺ 😐 ☹

Pool ☺ 😐 ☹ Hot Tub ☺ 😐 ☹

Places Visited / Activities:

People Met / New Friends:

Food, Dining & Restaurants:

Highlights / Memorable Events:

Places To Go & Things To Do for Next Time:

Notes:

Date: ____________

Weather:

From: ____________

To: ____________

Route Taken: ____________

Beginning Mileage: ____________

Ending Mileage: ____________

Total Miles Traveled:

Campground Information

Name: ____________

Address: ____________

Phone: ____________

Site # ________ $ ________ ☐ Day ☐ Week ☐ Month

☐ First Visit	☐ Return Visit	☐ Easy Access	
☐ Site Level	☐ Back-in	☐ Pull-through	
☐ 15 amp	☐ 30 amp	☐ 50 amp	
☐ Water	☐ Sewer	☐ Shade	☐ Sun
☐ Paved	☐ Sand / Grass	☐ Gravel	
☐ Picnic Table	☐ Fire ring	☐ Trees	☐ Lawn
☐ Patio	☐ Kid Friendly	☐ Pet Friendly	
☐ Store	☐ Cafe	☐ Firewood	
☐ Ice	☐ Security	☐ Quiet	☐ Noisy

Our Rating: ☆ ☆ ☆ ☆ ☆

GPS: ____________

Altitude: ____________

Cell Service / Carrier: ____________

☐ Antenna Reception ☐ Satellite TV ☐ Cable TV

☐ WIFI Available ☐ Free ☐ Fee $ ________

Memberships: ____________

Amenities: ____________

Location	☺	😐	☹	Water Pressure	☺	😐	☹
Restrooms	☺	😐	☹	Laundry	☺	😐	☹
Pool	☺	😐	☹	Hot Tub	☺	😐	☹

Places Visited / Activities:

People Met / New Friends:

Food, Dining & Restaurants:

Highlights / Memorable Events:

Places To Go & Things To Do for Next Time:

Notes:

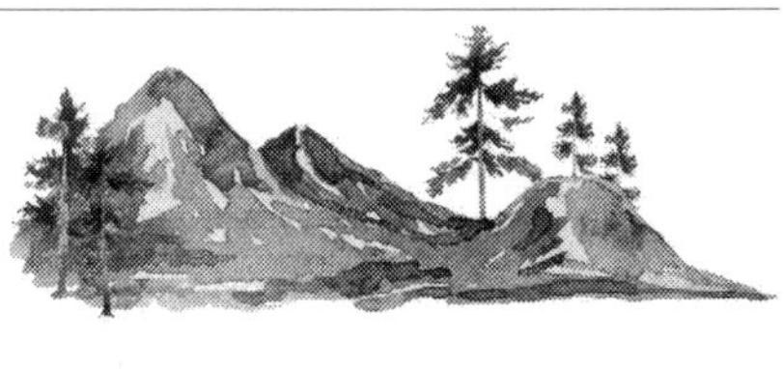

Date: ____	From: ____	Beginning Mileage: ____
Weather:	To: ____	Ending Mileage: ____
	Route Taken: ____	Total Miles Traveled:

Campground Information

Name: ____			Our Rating: ☆ ☆ ☆ ☆ ☆	
Address: ____			GPS: ____	
Phone: ____			Altitude: ____	
Site # ____	$ ____	☐ Day ☐ Week ☐ Month	Cell Service / Carrier: ____	
☐ First Visit	☐ Return Visit	☐ Easy Access	☐ Antenna Reception	☐ Satellite TV ☐ Cable TV
☐ Site Level	☐ Back-in	☐ Pull-through	☐ WIFI Available	☐ Free ☐ Fee $ ____
☐ 15 amp	☐ 30 amp	☐ 50 amp	Memberships: ____	
☐ Water	☐ Sewer	☐ Shade ☐ Sun	Amenities: ____	
☐ Paved	☐ Sand / Grass	☐ Gravel		
☐ Picnic Table	☐ Fire ring	☐ Trees ☐ Lawn	Location ☺ 😐 ☹	Water Pressure ☺ 😐 ☹
☐ Patio	☐ Kid Friendly	☐ Pet Friendly	Restrooms ☺ 😐 ☹	Laundry ☺ 😐 ☹
☐ Store	☐ Cafe	☐ Firewood	Pool ☺ 😐 ☹	Hot Tub ☺ 😐 ☹
☐ Ice	☐ Security	☐ Quiet ☐ Noisy		

Places Visited / Activities: ____

People Met / New Friends: ____

Food, Dining & Restaurants: ____

Highlights / Memorable Events: ____

Places To Go & Things To Do for Next Time: ____

Notes:

Date: ______	From: ______	Beginning Mileage: ______
Weather:	To: ______	Ending Mileage: ______
	Route Taken: ______	Total Miles Traveled:

Campground Information

Name: ______	Our Rating: ☆ ☆ ☆ ☆ ☆
Address: ______	GPS: ______
Phone: ______	Altitude: ______
Site # ______ $ ______ ☐ Day ☐ Week ☐ Month	Cell Service / Carrier: ______
☐ First Visit ☐ Return Visit ☐ Easy Access	☐ Antenna Reception ☐ Satellite TV ☐ Cable TV
☐ Site Level ☐ Back-in ☐ Pull-through	☐ WIFI Available ☐ Free ☐ Fee $ ______
☐ 15 amp ☐ 30 amp ☐ 50 amp	
☐ Water ☐ Sewer ☐ Shade ☐ Sun	Memberships: ______
☐ Paved ☐ Sand / Grass ☐ Gravel	Amenities: ______
☐ Picnic Table ☐ Fire ring ☐ Trees ☐ Lawn	
☐ Patio ☐ Kid Friendly ☐ Pet Friendly	Location ☺ 😐 ☹ Water Pressure ☺ 😐 ☹
☐ Store ☐ Cafe ☐ Firewood	Restrooms ☺ 😐 ☹ Laundry ☺ 😐 ☹
☐ Ice ☐ Security ☐ Quiet ☐ Noisy	Pool ☺ 😐 ☹ Hot Tub ☺ 😐 ☹

Places Visited / Activities: ______

People Met / New Friends: ______

Food, Dining & Restaurants: ______

Highlights / Memorable Events: ______

Places To Go & Things To Do for Next Time: ______

Notes:

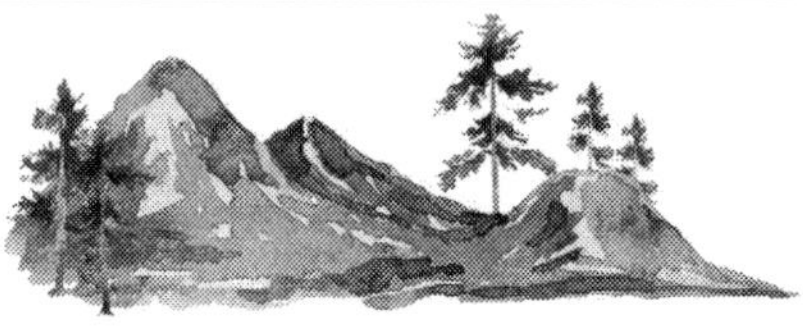

Date:	From:	Beginning Mileage:
Weather:	To:	Ending Mileage:
	Route Taken:	Total Miles Traveled:

Campground Information

Name:	Our Rating: ☆ ☆ ☆ ☆ ☆
Address:	GPS:
Phone:	Altitude:
Site # $ ☐ Day ☐ Week ☐ Month	Cell Service / Carrier:

- ☐ First Visit ☐ Return Visit ☐ Easy Access
- ☐ Site Level ☐ Back-in ☐ Pull-through
- ☐ 15 amp ☐ 30 amp ☐ 50 amp
- ☐ Water ☐ Sewer ☐ Shade ☐ Sun
- ☐ Paved ☐ Sand / Grass ☐ Gravel
- ☐ Picnic Table ☐ Fire ring ☐ Trees ☐ Lawn
- ☐ Patio ☐ Kid Friendly ☐ Pet Friendly
- ☐ Store ☐ Cafe ☐ Firewood
- ☐ Ice ☐ Security ☐ Quiet ☐ Noisy

- ☐ Antenna Reception ☐ Satellite TV ☐ Cable TV
- ☐ WIFI Available ☐ Free ☐ Fee $

Memberships:

Amenities:

Location	☺	😐	☹	Water Pressure	☺	😐	☹
Restrooms	☺	😐	☹	Laundry	☺	😐	☹
Pool	☺	😐	☹	Hot Tub	☺	😐	☹

Places Visited / Activities:

People Met / New Friends:

Food, Dining & Restaurants:

Highlights / Memorable Events:

Places To Go & Things To Do for Next Time:

NOTES:

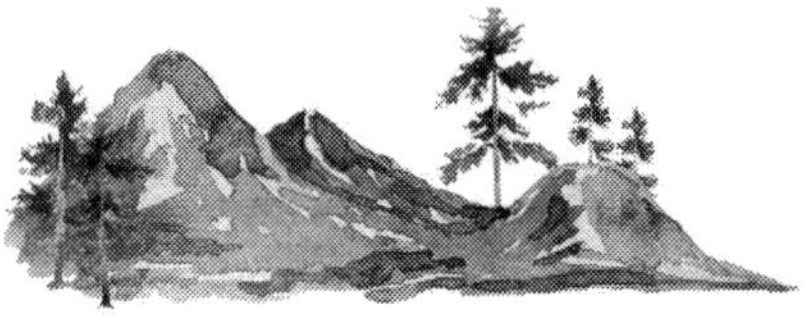

Date: ______	From: ______	Beginning Mileage: ______
Weather:	To: ______	Ending Mileage: ______
	Route Taken: ______	Total Miles Traveled:

Campground Information

Name: ______			
Address: ______			
Phone: ______			
Site # ______	$ ______	☐ Day ☐ Week	☐ Month
☐ First Visit	☐ Return Visit	☐ Easy Access	
☐ Site Level	☐ Back-in	☐ Pull-through	
☐ 15 amp	☐ 30 amp	☐ 50 amp	
☐ Water	☐ Sewer	☐ Shade	☐ Sun
☐ Paved	☐ Sand / Grass	☐ Gravel	
☐ Picnic Table	☐ Fire ring	☐ Trees	☐ Lawn
☐ Patio	☐ Kid Friendly	☐ Pet Friendly	
☐ Store	☐ Cafe	☐ Firewood	
☐ Ice	☐ Security	☐ Quiet	☐ Noisy

Our Rating: ☆ ☆ ☆ ☆ ☆

GPS: ______

Altitude: ______

Cell Service / Carrier: ______

☐ Antenna Reception ☐ Satellite TV ☐ Cable TV

☐ WIFI Available ☐ Free ☐ Fee $ ______

Memberships: ______

Amenities: ______

Location	☺	😐	☹	Water Pressure	☺	😐	☹
Restrooms	☺	😐	☹	Laundry	☺	😐	☹
Pool	☺	😐	☹	Hot Tub	☺	😐	☹

Places Visited / Activities:

People Met / New Friends:

Food, Dining & Restaurants:

Highlights / Memorable Events:

Places To Go & Things To Do for Next Time:

Notes:

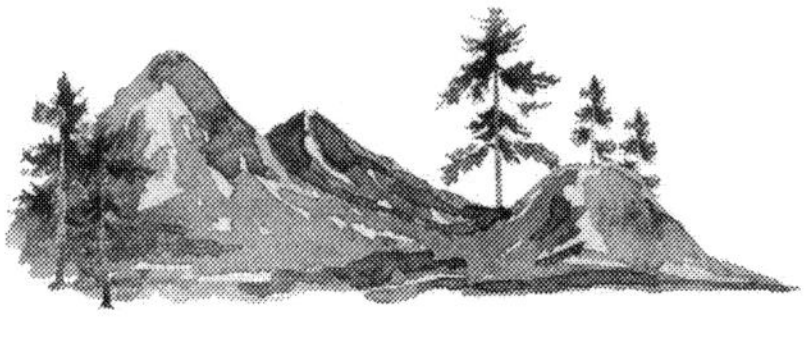

Date: ____	From: ____	Beginning Mileage: ____
Weather:	To: ____	Ending Mileage: ____
	Route Taken: ____	Total Miles Traveled:

Campground Information

Name:		Our Rating: ☆ ☆ ☆ ☆ ☆	
Address:		GPS:	
Phone:		Altitude:	
Site # ____ $ ____ ☐ Day ☐ Week ☐ Month		Cell Service / Carrier:	

☐ First Visit	☐ Return Visit	☐ Easy Access	
☐ Site Level	☐ Back-in	☐ Pull-through	
☐ 15 amp	☐ 30 amp	☐ 50 amp	
☐ Water	☐ Sewer	☐ Shade	☐ Sun
☐ Paved	☐ Sand / Grass	☐ Gravel	
☐ Picnic Table	☐ Fire ring	☐ Trees	☐ Lawn
☐ Patio	☐ Kid Friendly	☐ Pet Friendly	
☐ Store	☐ Cafe	☐ Firewood	
☐ Ice	☐ Security	☐ Quiet	☐ Noisy

☐ Antenna Reception ☐ Satellite TV ☐ Cable TV

☐ WIFI Available ☐ Free ☐ Fee $ ____

Memberships:

Amenities:

Location	☺	😐	☹	Water Pressure	☺	😐	☹
Restrooms	☺	😐	☹	Laundry	☺	😐	☹
Pool	☺	😐	☹	Hot Tub	☺	😐	☹

Places Visited / Activities:

People Met / New Friends:

Food, Dining & Restaurants:

Highlights / Memorable Events:

Places To Go & Things To Do for Next Time:

NOTES:

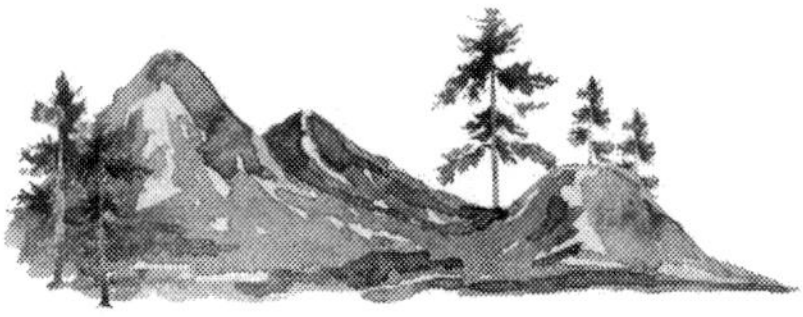

Date: ____________

Weather:

From: ____________

To: ____________

Route Taken: ____________

Beginning Mileage: ____________

Ending Mileage: ____________

Total Miles Traveled:

Campground Information

Name: ____________

Address: ____________

Phone: ____________

Site # ________ $ ________ ☐ Day ☐ Week ☐ Month

☐ First Visit	☐ Return Visit	☐ Easy Access	
☐ Site Level	☐ Back-in	☐ Pull-through	
☐ 15 amp	☐ 30 amp	☐ 50 amp	
☐ Water	☐ Sewer	☐ Shade	☐ Sun
☐ Paved	☐ Sand / Grass	☐ Gravel	
☐ Picnic Table	☐ Fire ring	☐ Trees	☐ Lawn
☐ Patio	☐ Kid Friendly	☐ Pet Friendly	
☐ Store	☐ Cafe	☐ Firewood	
☐ Ice	☐ Security	☐ Quiet	☐ Noisy

Our Rating: ☆ ☆ ☆ ☆ ☆

GPS: ____________

Altitude: ____________

Cell Service / Carrier: ____________

☐ Antenna Reception ☐ Satellite TV ☐ Cable TV

☐ WIFI Available ☐ Free ☐ Fee $ ________

Memberships: ____________

Amenities: ____________

Location	☺ 😐 ☹	Water Pressure	☺ 😐 ☹
Restrooms	☺ 😐 ☹	Laundry	☺ 😐 ☹
Pool	☺ 😐 ☹	Hot Tub	☺ 😐 ☹

Places Visited / Activities:

People Met / New Friends:

Food, Dining & Restaurants:

Highlights / Memorable Events:

Places To Go & Things To Do for Next Time:

Notes:

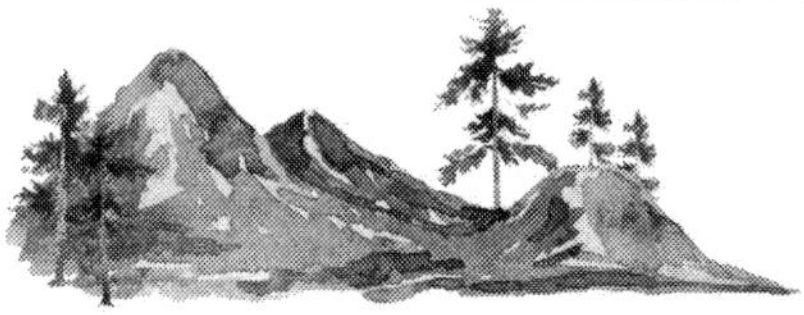

Date:	From:	Beginning Mileage:
Weather:	To:	Ending Mileage:
	Route Taken:	Total Miles Traveled:

Campground Information

Name:

Address:

Phone:

Site # ______ $ ______ ☐ Day ☐ Week ☐ Month

☐ First Visit	☐ Return Visit	☐ Easy Access	
☐ Site Level	☐ Back-in	☐ Pull-through	
☐ 15 amp	☐ 30 amp	☐ 50 amp	
☐ Water	☐ Sewer	☐ Shade	☐ Sun
☐ Paved	☐ Sand / Grass	☐ Gravel	
☐ Picnic Table	☐ Fire ring	☐ Trees	☐ Lawn
☐ Patio	☐ Kid Friendly	☐ Pet Friendly	
☐ Store	☐ Cafe	☐ Firewood	
☐ Ice	☐ Security	☐ Quiet	☐ Noisy

Our Rating: ☆ ☆ ☆ ☆ ☆

GPS:

Altitude:

Cell Service / Carrier:

☐ Antenna Reception ☐ Satellite TV ☐ Cable TV

☐ WIFI Available ☐ Free ☐ Fee $

Memberships:

Amenities:

Location	☺	😐	☹	Water Pressure	☺	😐	☹
Restrooms	☺	😐	☹	Laundry	☺	😐	☹
Pool	☺	😐	☹	Hot Tub	☺	😐	☹

Places Visited / Activities:

People Met / New Friends:

Food, Dining & Restaurants:

Highlights / Memorable Events:

Places To Go & Things To Do for Next Time:

Notes:

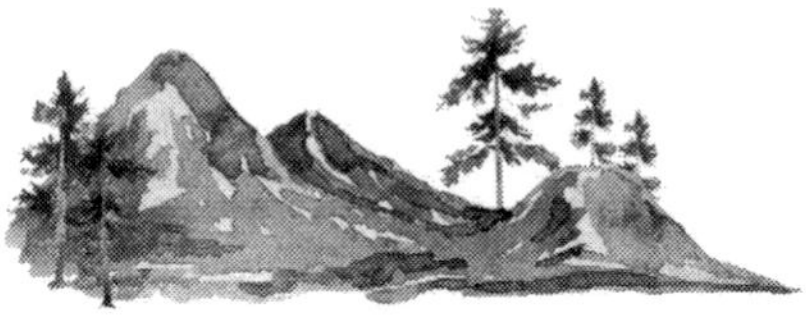

Date: ______

Weather:

From: ______

To: ______

Route Taken: ______

Beginning Mileage: ______

Ending Mileage: ______

Total Miles Traveled:

Campground Information

Name: ______

Address: ______

Phone: ______

Site # ______ $ ______ ☐ Day ☐ Week ☐ Month

☐ First Visit ☐ Return Visit ☐ Easy Access
☐ Site Level ☐ Back-in ☐ Pull-through
☐ 15 amp ☐ 30 amp ☐ 50 amp
☐ Water ☐ Sewer ☐ Shade ☐ Sun
☐ Paved ☐ Sand / Grass ☐ Gravel
☐ Picnic Table ☐ Fire ring ☐ Trees ☐ Lawn
☐ Patio ☐ Kid Friendly ☐ Pet Friendly
☐ Store ☐ Cafe ☐ Firewood
☐ Ice ☐ Security ☐ Quiet ☐ Noisy

Our Rating: ☆ ☆ ☆ ☆ ☆

GPS: ______

Altitude: ______

Cell Service / Carrier: ______

☐ Antenna Reception ☐ Satellite TV ☐ Cable TV
☐ WIFI Available ☐ Free ☐ Fee $ ______

Memberships: ______

Amenities: ______

Location	☺	😐	☹	Water Pressure	☺	😐	☹
Restrooms	☺	😐	☹	Laundry	☺	😐	☹
Pool	☺	😐	☹	Hot Tub	☺	😐	☹

Places Visited / Activities:

People Met / New Friends:

Food, Dining & Restaurants:

Highlights / Memorable Events:

Places To Go & Things To Do for Next Time:

Notes:

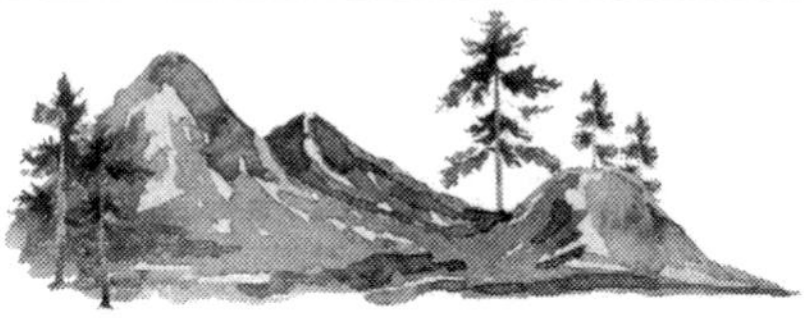

Date: ____________

Weather:

From: ____________

To: ____________

Route Taken: ____________

Beginning Mileage: ____________

Ending Mileage: ____________

Total Miles Traveled:

Campground Information

Name: ____________

Address: ____________

Phone: ____________

Site # ________ $ ________ ☐ Day ☐ Week ☐ Month

☐ First Visit	☐ Return Visit	☐ Easy Access	
☐ Site Level	☐ Back-in	☐ Pull-through	
☐ 15 amp	☐ 30 amp	☐ 50 amp	
☐ Water	☐ Sewer	☐ Shade	☐ Sun
☐ Paved	☐ Sand / Grass	☐ Gravel	
☐ Picnic Table	☐ Fire ring	☐ Trees	☐ Lawn
☐ Patio	☐ Kid Friendly	☐ Pet Friendly	
☐ Store	☐ Cafe	☐ Firewood	
☐ Ice	☐ Security	☐ Quiet	☐ Noisy

Our Rating: ☆ ☆ ☆ ☆ ☆

GPS: ____________

Altitude: ____________

Cell Service / Carrier: ____________

☐ Antenna Reception ☐ Satellite TV ☐ Cable TV

☐ WIFI Available ☐ Free ☐ Fee $ ________

Memberships: ____________

Amenities: ____________

Location	☺	😐	☹	Water Pressure	☺	😐	☹
Restrooms	☺	😐	☹	Laundry	☺	😐	☹
Pool	☺	😐	☹	Hot Tub	☺	😐	☹

Places Visited / Activities:

People Met / New Friends:

Food, Dining & Restaurants:

Highlights / Memorable Events:

Places To Go & Things To Do for Next Time:

Notes:

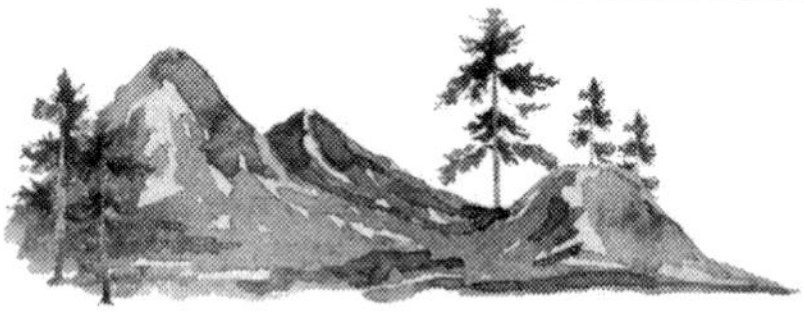

Date:

Weather:

From:

To:

Route Taken:

Beginning Mileage:

Ending Mileage:

Total Miles Traveled:

Campground Information

Name:

Address:

Phone:

Site # $ ☐ Day ☐ Week ☐ Month

☐ First Visit ☐ Return Visit ☐ Easy Access

☐ Site Level ☐ Back-in ☐ Pull-through

☐ 15 amp ☐ 30 amp ☐ 50 amp

☐ Water ☐ Sewer ☐ Shade ☐ Sun

☐ Paved ☐ Sand / Grass ☐ Gravel

☐ Picnic Table ☐ Fire ring ☐ Trees ☐ Lawn

☐ Patio ☐ Kid Friendly ☐ Pet Friendly

☐ Store ☐ Cafe ☐ Firewood

☐ Ice ☐ Security ☐ Quiet ☐ Noisy

Our Rating: ☆ ☆ ☆ ☆ ☆

GPS:

Altitude:

Cell Service / Carrier:

☐ Antenna Reception ☐ Satellite TV ☐ Cable TV

☐ WIFI Available ☐ Free ☐ Fee $

Memberships:

Amenities:

Location

Restrooms

Pool

Water Pressure

Laundry

Hot Tub

Places Visited / Activities:

People Met / New Friends:

Food, Dining & Restaurants:

Highlights / Memorable Events:

Places To Go & Things To Do for Next Time:

Notes:

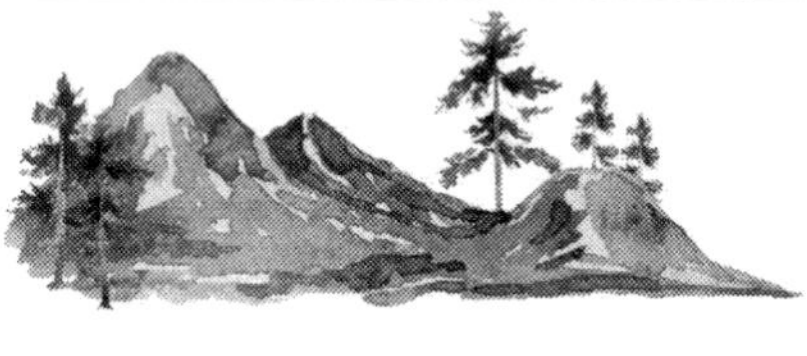

Date:

Weather:

From:

To:

Route Taken:

Beginning Mileage:

Ending Mileage:

Total Miles Traveled:

Campground Information

Name:

Address:

Phone:

Site # ______ $ ______ ☐ Day ☐ Week ☐ Month

☐ First Visit	☐ Return Visit	☐ Easy Access	
☐ Site Level	☐ Back-in	☐ Pull-through	
☐ 15 amp	☐ 30 amp	☐ 50 amp	
☐ Water	☐ Sewer	☐ Shade	☐ Sun
☐ Paved	☐ Sand / Grass	☐ Gravel	
☐ Picnic Table	☐ Fire ring	☐ Trees	☐ Lawn
☐ Patio	☐ Kid Friendly	☐ Pet Friendly	
☐ Store	☐ Cafe	☐ Firewood	
☐ Ice	☐ Security	☐ Quiet	☐ Noisy

Our Rating: ☆ ☆ ☆ ☆ ☆

GPS:

Altitude:

Cell Service / Carrier:

☐ Antenna Reception ☐ Satellite TV ☐ Cable TV

☐ WIFI Available ☐ Free ☐ Fee $

Memberships:

Amenities:

Location	☺ 😐 ☹	Water Pressure ☺ 😐 ☹
Restrooms	☺ 😐 ☹	Laundry ☺ 😐 ☹
Pool	☺ 😐 ☹	Hot Tub ☺ 😐 ☹

Places Visited / Activities:

People Met / New Friends:

Food, Dining & Restaurants:

Highlights / Memorable Events:

Places To Go & Things To Do for Next Time:

NOTES:

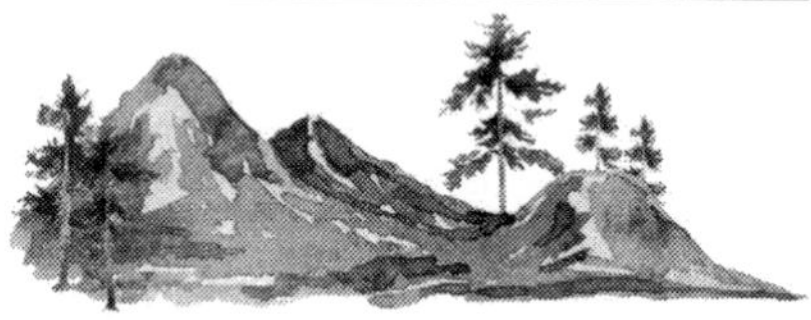

Date: ____________

Weather:

From: ____________

To: ____________

Route Taken: ____________

Beginning Mileage: ____________

Ending Mileage: ____________

Total Miles Traveled:

Campground Information

Name: ____________

Address: ____________

Phone: ____________

Site # ________ $ ________ ☐ Day ☐ Week ☐ Month

☐ First Visit ☐ Return Visit ☐ Easy Access

☐ Site Level ☐ Back-in ☐ Pull-through

☐ 15 amp ☐ 30 amp ☐ 50 amp

☐ Water ☐ Sewer ☐ Shade ☐ Sun

☐ Paved ☐ Sand / Grass ☐ Gravel

☐ Picnic Table ☐ Fire ring ☐ Trees ☐ Lawn

☐ Patio ☐ Kid Friendly ☐ Pet Friendly

☐ Store ☐ Cafe ☐ Firewood

☐ Ice ☐ Security ☐ Quiet ☐ Noisy

Our Rating: ☆ ☆ ☆ ☆ ☆

GPS: ____________

Altitude: ____________

Cell Service / Carrier: ____________

☐ Antenna Reception ☐ Satellite TV ☐ Cable TV

☐ WIFI Available ☐ Free ☐ Fee $ ________

Memberships: ____________

Amenities: ____________

Location ☺ 😐 ☹ Water Pressure ☺ 😐 ☹

Restrooms ☺ 😐 ☹ Laundry ☺ 😐 ☹

Pool ☺ 😐 ☹ Hot Tub ☺ 😐 ☹

Places Visited / Activities:

People Met / New Friends:

Food, Dining & Restaurants:

Highlights / Memorable Events:

Places To Go & Things To Do for Next Time:

Notes:

Date: ______________________

Weather:

From: ______________________

To: ______________________

Route Taken: ______________________

Beginning Mileage: ______________________

Ending Mileage: ______________________

Total Miles Traveled:

Campground Information

Name: ______________________

Address: ______________________

Phone: ______________________

Site # __________ $ __________ ☐ Day ☐ Week ☐ Month

☐ First Visit	☐ Return Visit	☐ Easy Access	
☐ Site Level	☐ Back-in	☐ Pull-through	
☐ 15 amp	☐ 30 amp	☐ 50 amp	
☐ Water	☐ Sewer	☐ Shade	☐ Sun
☐ Paved	☐ Sand / Grass	☐ Gravel	
☐ Picnic Table	☐ Fire ring	☐ Trees	☐ Lawn
☐ Patio	☐ Kid Friendly	☐ Pet Friendly	
☐ Store	☐ Cafe	☐ Firewood	
☐ Ice	☐ Security	☐ Quiet	☐ Noisy

Our Rating: ☆ ☆ ☆ ☆ ☆

GPS: ______________________

Altitude: ______________________

Cell Service / Carrier: ______________________

☐ Antenna Reception ☐ Satellite TV ☐ Cable TV

☐ WIFI Available ☐ Free ☐ Fee $ __________

Memberships: ______________________

Amenities: ______________________

Location	☺	😐	☹	Water Pressure	☺	😐	☹
Restrooms	☺	😐	☹	Laundry	☺	😐	☹
Pool	☺	😐	☹	Hot Tub	☺	😐	☹

Places Visited / Activities:

People Met / New Friends:

Food, Dining & Restaurants:

Highlights / Memorable Events:

Places To Go & Things To Do for Next Time:

Notes:

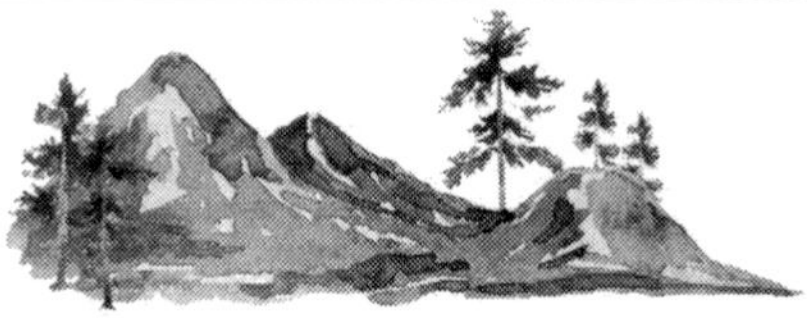

Date: ____________

Weather:

From: ____________

To: ____________

Route Taken: ____________

Beginning Mileage:

Ending Mileage:

Total Miles Traveled:

Campground Information

Name: ____________

Address: ____________

Phone: ____________

Site # ________ $ ________ ☐ Day ☐ Week ☐ Month

☐ First Visit ☐ Return Visit ☐ Easy Access

☐ Site Level ☐ Back-in ☐ Pull-through

☐ 15 amp ☐ 30 amp ☐ 50 amp

☐ Water ☐ Sewer ☐ Shade ☐ Sun

☐ Paved ☐ Sand / Grass ☐ Gravel

☐ Picnic Table ☐ Fire ring ☐ Trees ☐ Lawn

☐ Patio ☐ Kid Friendly ☐ Pet Friendly

☐ Store ☐ Cafe ☐ Firewood

☐ Ice ☐ Security ☐ Quiet ☐ Noisy

Our Rating: ☆ ☆ ☆ ☆ ☆

GPS: ____________

Altitude: ____________

Cell Service / Carrier: ____________

☐ Antenna Reception ☐ Satellite TV ☐ Cable TV

☐ WIFI Available ☐ Free ☐ Fee $ ________

Memberships: ____________

Amenities: ____________

Location ☺ 😐 ☹ Water Pressure ☺ 😐 ☹

Restrooms ☺ 😐 ☹ Laundry ☺ 😐 ☹

Pool ☺ 😐 ☹ Hot Tub ☺ 😐 ☹

Places Visited / Activities:

People Met / New Friends:

Food, Dining & Restaurants:

Highlights / Memorable Events:

Places To Go & Things To Do for Next Time:

Notes:

Date: ______

Weather:

From: ______

To: ______

Route Taken: ______

Beginning Mileage: ______

Ending Mileage: ______

Total Miles Traveled:

Campground Information

Name: ______

Address: ______

Phone: ______

Site # ______ $ ______ ☐ Day ☐ Week ☐ Month

☐ First Visit ☐ Return Visit ☐ Easy Access

☐ Site Level ☐ Back-in ☐ Pull-through

☐ 15 amp ☐ 30 amp ☐ 50 amp

☐ Water ☐ Sewer ☐ Shade ☐ Sun

☐ Paved ☐ Sand / Grass ☐ Gravel

☐ Picnic Table ☐ Fire ring ☐ Trees ☐ Lawn

☐ Patio ☐ Kid Friendly ☐ Pet Friendly

☐ Store ☐ Cafe ☐ Firewood

☐ Ice ☐ Security ☐ Quiet ☐ Noisy

Our Rating: ☆ ☆ ☆ ☆ ☆

GPS: ______

Altitude: ______

Cell Service / Carrier: ______

☐ Antenna Reception ☐ Satellite TV ☐ Cable TV

☐ WIFI Available ☐ Free ☐ Fee $ ______

Memberships: ______

Amenities: ______

Location	☺	😐	☹	Water Pressure	☺	😐	☹
Restrooms	☺	😐	☹	Laundry	☺	😐	☹
Pool	☺	😐	☹	Hot Tub	☺	😐	☹

Places Visited / Activities:

People Met / New Friends:

Food, Dining & Restaurants:

Highlights / Memorable Events:

Places To Go & Things To Do for Next Time:

Notes:

Date:

Weather:

From:

To:

Route Taken:

Beginning Mileage:

Ending Mileage:

Total Miles Traveled:

Campground Information

Name:

Address:

Phone:

Site # $ ☐ Day ☐ Week ☐ Month

☐ First Visit	☐ Return Visit	☐ Easy Access	
☐ Site Level	☐ Back-in	☐ Pull-through	
☐ 15 amp	☐ 30 amp	☐ 50 amp	
☐ Water	☐ Sewer	☐ Shade	☐ Sun
☐ Paved	☐ Sand / Grass	☐ Gravel	
☐ Picnic Table	☐ Fire ring	☐ Trees	☐ Lawn
☐ Patio	☐ Kid Friendly	☐ Pet Friendly	
☐ Store	☐ Cafe	☐ Firewood	
☐ Ice	☐ Security	☐ Quiet	☐ Noisy

Our Rating: ☆ ☆ ☆ ☆ ☆

GPS:

Altitude:

Cell Service / Carrier:

☐ Antenna Reception ☐ Satellite TV ☐ Cable TV

☐ WIFI Available ☐ Free ☐ Fee $

Memberships:

Amenities:

Location	☺ 😐 ☹	Water Pressure	☺ 😐 ☹
Restrooms	☺ 😐 ☹	Laundry	☺ 😐 ☹
Pool	☺ 😐 ☹	Hot Tub	☺ 😐 ☹

Places Visited / Activities:

People Met / New Friends:

Food, Dining & Restaurants:

Highlights / Memorable Events:

Places To Go & Things To Do for Next Time:

Notes:

Date: ______	From: ______	Beginning Mileage: ______
Weather:	To: ______	Ending Mileage: ______
	Route Taken: ______	Total Miles Traveled:

Campground Information

Name: ______	Our Rating: ☆ ☆ ☆ ☆ ☆
Address: ______	GPS: ______
Phone: ______	Altitude: ______
Site # ______ $ ______ ☐ Day ☐ Week ☐ Month	Cell Service / Carrier: ______
☐ First Visit ☐ Return Visit ☐ Easy Access	☐ Antenna Reception ☐ Satellite TV ☐ Cable TV
☐ Site Level ☐ Back-in ☐ Pull-through	☐ WIFI Available ☐ Free ☐ Fee $ ______
☐ 15 amp ☐ 30 amp ☐ 50 amp	
☐ Water ☐ Sewer ☐ Shade ☐ Sun	Memberships: ______
☐ Paved ☐ Sand / Grass ☐ Gravel	Amenities: ______
☐ Picnic Table ☐ Fire ring ☐ Trees ☐ Lawn	Location ☺ 😐 ☹ Water Pressure ☺ 😐 ☹
☐ Patio ☐ Kid Friendly ☐ Pet Friendly	Restrooms ☺ 😐 ☹ Laundry ☺ 😐 ☹
☐ Store ☐ Cafe ☐ Firewood	
☐ Ice ☐ Security ☐ Quiet ☐ Noisy	Pool ☺ 😐 ☹ Hot Tub ☺ 😐 ☹

Places Visited / Activities: ______

People Met / New Friends: ______

Food, Dining & Restaurants: ______

Highlights / Memorable Events: ______

Places To Go & Things To Do for Next Time: ______

Notes:

Date: ______ Weather:	From: ______ To: ______ Route Taken: ______	Beginning Mileage: ______ Ending Mileage: ______ Total Miles Traveled:

Campground Information

Name: ______

Address: ______

Phone: ______

Site # ______ $ ______ ☐ Day ☐ Week ☐ Month

☐ First Visit	☐ Return Visit	☐ Easy Access	
☐ Site Level	☐ Back-in	☐ Pull-through	
☐ 15 amp	☐ 30 amp	☐ 50 amp	
☐ Water	☐ Sewer	☐ Shade	☐ Sun
☐ Paved	☐ Sand / Grass	☐ Gravel	
☐ Picnic Table	☐ Fire ring	☐ Trees	☐ Lawn
☐ Patio	☐ Kid Friendly	☐ Pet Friendly	
☐ Store	☐ Cafe	☐ Firewood	
☐ Ice	☐ Security	☐ Quiet	☐ Noisy

Our Rating: ☆ ☆ ☆ ☆ ☆

GPS: ______

Altitude: ______

Cell Service / Carrier: ______

☐ Antenna Reception ☐ Satellite TV ☐ Cable TV

☐ WIFI Available ☐ Free ☐ Fee $ ______

Memberships: ______

Amenities: ______

Location	☺	😐	☹	Water Pressure	☺	😐	☹
Restrooms	☺	😐	☹	Laundry	☺	😐	☹
Pool	☺	😐	☹	Hot Tub	☺	😐	☹

Places Visited / Activities:

People Met / New Friends:

Food, Dining & Restaurants:

Highlights / Memorable Events:

Places To Go & Things To Do for Next Time:

Notes:

Date: ____	From: ____	Beginning Mileage: ____
Weather:	To: ____	Ending Mileage: ____
	Route Taken: ____	Total Miles Traveled:

Campground Information

Name: ____	Our Rating: ☆ ☆ ☆ ☆ ☆
Address: ____	GPS: ____
Phone: ____	Altitude: ____
Site # ____ $ ____ ☐ Day ☐ Week ☐ Month	Cell Service / Carrier: ____
☐ First Visit ☐ Return Visit ☐ Easy Access	☐ Antenna Reception ☐ Satellite TV ☐ Cable TV
☐ Site Level ☐ Back-in ☐ Pull-through	☐ WIFI Available ☐ Free ☐ Fee $ ____
☐ 15 amp ☐ 30 amp ☐ 50 amp	
☐ Water ☐ Sewer ☐ Shade ☐ Sun	Memberships: ____
☐ Paved ☐ Sand / Grass ☐ Gravel	Amenities: ____
☐ Picnic Table ☐ Fire ring ☐ Trees ☐ Lawn	Location ☺ 😐 ☹ Water Pressure ☺ 😐 ☹
☐ Patio ☐ Kid Friendly ☐ Pet Friendly	Restrooms ☺ 😐 ☹ Laundry ☺ 😐 ☹
☐ Store ☐ Cafe ☐ Firewood	
☐ Ice ☐ Security ☐ Quiet ☐ Noisy	Pool ☺ 😐 ☹ Hot Tub ☺ 😐 ☹

Places Visited / Activities:

People Met / New Friends:

Food, Dining & Restaurants:

Highlights / Memorable Events:

Places To Go & Things To Do for Next Time:

NOTES:

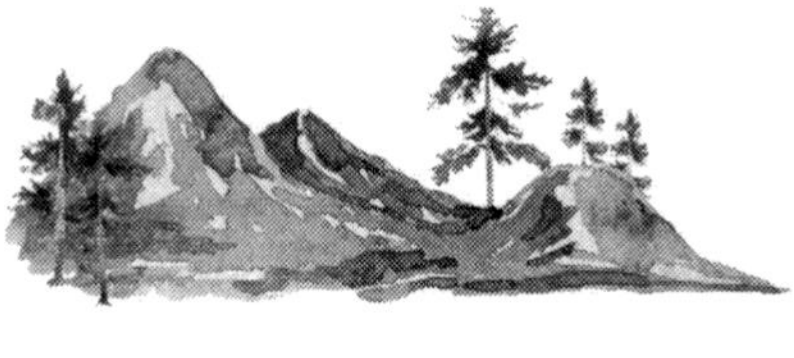

Made in the USA
Monee, IL
27 August 2022

1a4d5e83-9b7c-44f8-bca3-e047aff4515fR01